Music and Technology: A Very Short Introduction

VERY SHORT INTRODUCTIONS are for anyone wanting a stimulating and accessible way into a new subject. They are written by experts, and have been translated into more than 45 different languages.

The series began in 1995, and now covers a wide variety of topics in every discipline. The VSI library currently contains over 700 volumes—a Very Short Introduction to everything from Psychology and Philosophy of Science to American History and Relativity—and continues to grow in every subject area.

Very Short Introductions available now:

Available soon:

For more information visit our website

www.oup.com/vsi/

Mark Katz

MUSIC AND TECHNOLOGY

A Very Short Introduction

OXFORD
UNIVERSITY PRESS

OXFORD
UNIVERSITY PRESS

Oxford University Press is a department of the University of Oxford.
It furthers the University's objective of excellence in research, scholarship,
and education by publishing worldwide. Oxford is a registered trade mark of
Oxford University Press in the UK and certain other countries.

Published in the United States of America by Oxford University Press
198 Madison Avenue, New York, NY 10016, United States of America.

Library of Congress Cataloging-in-Publication Data

Names: Katz, Mark, 1970– author.
Title: Music and technology : a very short introduction / Mark Katz.
Description: New York : Oxford University Press, 2022. |
Series: Very short introductions
Identifiers: LCCN 2022006327 | ISBN 9780199946983 (paperback) |
ISBN 9780199947003 (epub)
Subjects: LCSH: Music and technology. | Music—Social aspects. | Sound
recordings—Social aspects. | Musical instruments.
Classification: LCC ML3916 .K38 2022 | DDC 780.285—dc23
LC record available at https://lccn.loc.gov/2022006327

1 3 5 7 9 8 6 4 2

Printed in the UK by Ashford Colour Press Ltd, Gosport, Hampshire.,
on acid-free paper

Contents

List of illustrations

Acknowledgments

This book has been in progress much longer than I expected. My first thanks, then, must go to my wonderful and patient editor at Oxford University Press, Nancy Toff. Over the years that this book has been gestating, many others have provided support, whether by offering feedback, providing research assistance, serving as an accountability partner, sharing their work, inviting me to present lectures on the subject of the book, or simply talking with me about music and technology. These generous and thoughtful people include Tuomas Auvinen, Paul Berliner, Andrea Bohlman, Mark Evan Bonds, John Caldwell, Melissa Camp, Will Cheng, Allison DiBianca, ken tianyuan Ge, Kjetil Falkenberg Hansen, Joanna Helms, Aldwyn Hogg Jr., Eri Kakoki, Jj Kidder, Stella Li, Sarah Lindmark, Michael Levine, Áine Mangaoang, Alex Marsden, John Richardson, Eduardo Sato, Kelli Smith-Biwer, Jason Stanyek, Tim Sterner Miller, Matthew Thibeault, David VanderHamm, and the two sets of anonymous readers who wrote helpful reports on the manuscript (ten years apart!). Dozens of students in a variety of classes at the University of North Carolina at Chapel Hill have also read parts of this book. Moreover, several graduate students (all named above) introduced me to some of the technologies and topics I discuss in this book. I cannot emphasize enough how valuable it is to have had so many smart students respond to my ideas and my writing; they have helped me make this a clearer, more interesting book, and I am deeply grateful. Above all, I owe my thanks to my wife, Beth Jakub, and my daughter, Anna Katz, who support me in every possible way and make everything better. This book is for them.

Chapter 1
Music as technology

"I'm so thankful I was a DJ before technology took over." Making the rounds on social media in early 2015, this wistful remark elicited the knowing approval of those who had witnessed wave after wave of technological change in the previous decade. The DJs who resented this apparent takeover had started their careers in the analog days of yore, mastering less user-friendly equipment and lugging heavy crates of vinyl discs from gig to gig. Since then, however, it had become markedly easier and cheaper to acquire, arrange, store, mix, edit, and reproduce recorded music—that is, to do the work of the DJ, or what used to be called a disc jockey. For many veteran DJs, these changes exposed technology's dark side: in simplifying their craft, it had also devalued their hard-won skill, labor, and experience.

The statement "I'm so thankful I was a DJ before technology took over" might seem nonsensical. After all, the DJ as we know it could not exist without electronic technologies. But this declaration is not so much a rejection of technology as it is an expression of ambivalence and anxiety, revealing a widely held concern that technology can be an intrusive, corrupting force. This is not a new sentiment. Consider the piano. In the eighteenth century it was an interloper when the harpsichord—an older keyboard instrument—ruled the concert halls and salons of Europe. In 1774, the French philosopher Voltaire dismissed the new keyboard as an *instrument du chaudronnier*—a metalworker's tool, hardly suitable for the art of music. A century later many cultures embraced the piano, and it was regarded as a traditional musical instrument. In 1906, the US bandleader and composer John Philip Sousa likened the now venerable piano to a native songbird menaced by an invasive species, here represented by the player piano, a new mechanical keyboard instrument in which scrolling rolls of perforated paper activated each note. What had changed since Voltaire's time? The piano had only become more complex, now an iron-encased marvel of keys, hammers, strings, pedals, dampers, jacks, and dozens of other moving parts. And yet, having become assimilated into musical and domestic life, it was no longer regarded as a form of technology. The piano had become as natural as a songbird. As it turns out, complaints about the takeover of technology are never about the tainting of some pretechnological state. Rather, they typically voice concerns about a new form of technology disrupting or threatening an established practice that employs older, familiar technologies.

Throughout history we see repeated cycles in which technologies are hypervisible as they are introduced into spheres of human activity and then become invisible once they are incorporated into regular use and are no longer noteworthy. Hypervisibility and invisibility both distort the influence of technology. When technologies are hypervisible we tend to exaggerate their impact and disregard the broader contexts that shape their use and give them meaning. Invisible technologies, however, are overlooked, their influence unappreciated. They are not even deemed technological.

Most of us encounter hypervisible and invisible technologies daily. If I stop typing and look at my desk, I notice a computer keyboard, monitor, and mouse; pens and pencils; some framed photos; a pad of sticky notes; a selection of books; my smartphone. All these objects are forms of technology, as are the desk itself and the chair underneath me. As unremarkable as it may seem, this assemblage of objects represents an extraordinary convergence of technologies from across ages and continents. Paper is 2,000 years old; the first known printed book dates to 868; the pencil was invented in 1795; the first photograph was taken in 1826; the ballpoint pen was created in 1938; the computer mouse was born in 1964; sticky notes came out in 1977; the smartphone was introduced in 1992. These technologies are as far-flung geographically as they are chronologically: paper and printed books originated in China; the pencil and photograph are French; the ballpoint pen is Hungarian; the mouse, sticky notes, and smartphone were developed in the United States. Try this yourself. What do you see? When we open our eyes to the varied origins, ages, contexts, and uses of the tools and devices around us we begin to understand the rich and complex ways that we interact with technology.

Defining music technology

This book embraces a broad understanding of technology, one that includes any tools or systems meant to transform human existence in some way. Music technology, then, encompasses tools and systems designed or used to facilitate the creation, preservation, reception, or dissemination of music. In this view, technologies of music not only include the usual suspects—devices that are new, complicated, and electronic—but also all instruments, however old or simple, as well as music notation and printing. The human body can also be considered a form of technology. When we make music with our mouths, lungs, and limbs, we manipulate our bodies as musical tools to create the sounds we desire. Singers often call their voices their instruments, and musical traditions around the world—among them African American Juba dance (or hambone) and the *palmas* of flamenco—treat bodies as percussion instruments by stomping, patting, clapping, and snapping. Musicians modify their bodies to serve their art as well. Some guitarists and banjo players grow out the fingernails of their right hand to serve as a plectrum, or pick, while many players of the sarod, a Hindustani stringed instrument, do the same with the nails of their left hand. Country music star Dolly

Parton has called her acrylic fingernails musical instruments, not only treating them as guitar picks but also using them to create percussive sounds of their own. At times, musicians' bodily modifications are more considerable, even irreversible. A castrato, for example, was a male singer castrated before puberty for the purpose of cultivating a high, flexible, and powerful voice that was prized in Europe for more than 300 years, well into the nineteenth century.

There are two main reasons for embracing such a broad definition of music technology. First, it allows us to see continuities and relationships obscured by the tendency to focus on the novel or disruptive aspects of technology. For example, sampling (the extraction and musical repurposing of fragments of existing recordings) and mashups (the combination of two or more recordings into a single piece) are developments of the digital age and have been considered both novel and disruptive. But they are not unprecedented—both are forms of musical quotation, a centuries-old practice. To see this connection is to understand not only that sampling and mashups are products of their times but also that they draw from a common well of creative impulses.

Second, an expansive view of technology can illuminate hidden cultural contexts and power dynamics. Technology is not an essence that inheres in some objects and not in others—it is a concept, a label that reflects values, norms, and biases. To describe something in technological terms is to recognize it and its creators as worthy of respect. In Western societies, the esteemed title of "inventor" has traditionally been reserved for white men. Women and people of color who have made similar contributions are less frequently recognized as inventors and are regularly denied access to technology. In music, this has meant that women composers and performers as well as nonwhite musicians have been shut out of recording and electronic music studios and their interests and needs dismissed by instrument and musical equipment manufacturers. A narrow definition of technology allows those in power and other self-appointed gatekeepers to exclude others. Definitions can have real-world consequences, and there is value in adopting ones that uncover hidden connections, recognize the cultural embeddedness of our inventions, and foster an appreciation of the incredible diversity of human musical ingenuity.

A very, very short history of music technology

The following very, very short history considers three areas of music technology: instruments, notation and printing, and sound recording and broadcast. This sketch cites well-known names and inventions as well as lesser-known developments, some modern technologies, and some ancient.

The earliest music technologies external to the human body probably emerged in the Paleolithic era. Sometime about 35,000 years ago one of our ancestors sat down with the wing bone of a vulture and made it into a flute. That flute, found in 2008 in a dozen pieces in a cave in southwestern Germany, features five precisely measured and finely cut finger holes over its approximately 8.5-inch (21.8-centimeter) length. It is clearly the work of a skilled, tool-using builder. Given that people at the time were preoccupied with gathering food, battling rival clans, and dodging cave bears, it is a testament to the power of music that such care would be lavished on bringing an instrument to life.

The tradition of instrument building is likely millennia older than this bone flute—it is merely the earliest known example at this time. We cannot know when people first made music, but fossil records show that humans have had the physical ability to sing for more than 500,000 years and have been using tools for at least 3 million years. Birds, by the way, have been singing for tens of millions of years and certainly inspired some of the earliest human music making. Countless instruments still in use in the early twenty-first century depend on animals for their construction. The shofar, Middle Eastern in origin and played on Jewish holy days, is a wind instrument made from a ram's or goat's horn; the bowed Chinese stringed instrument, the erhu, traditionally uses python skin to cover its wooden soundbox; bagpipes, common in Ireland and Scotland, have long incorporated cow, goat, or sheep skins. In recent decades, synthetics have replaced animal sources; as with all technological practices, instrument building evolves in response to changing values and aesthetics as well as the availability and development of tools and techniques. Since prehistoric times and continuing to this day, animals have served as a benchmark for our musicality and have given their lives to facilitate much of our music making.

Bone flutes and bagpipes are not usually cited as forms of technology, perhaps because of their use of natural materials. Classic examples of music technology tend to be mechanical or electronic musical instruments, but they are neither fundamentally different nor particularly new.

The player piano—an uncanny device invented in the nineteenth century that can perform without a human operator—is a canonic form of music technology. It is also part of an ancient tradition of musical automata. The earliest examples were probably flutes or organs driven by continuously flowing water cited in Greek sources from the third century BCE. In 850, a trio of scientist brothers working in Baghdad known as the Banū Mūsà described a water-powered organ and a hydraulically blown flute in their book, *Kitāb al-Ḥiyal*, or the *Book of Ingenious Devices*. Some sixteenth- and seventeenth-century water-powered organs in Europe were still being played in the twenty-first century, such as the 1502 instrument in Hohensalzburg Castle in Austria and the 1549 organ at the Villa d'Este in Tivoli, outside Rome. Starting in the fifteenth century, most automatic instruments were driven by spring-powered mechanisms, the kind developed out of early clockwork technology. The heyday of musical automata has long passed, but the technology continues to delight and discomfit, whether in the form of music boxes gifted on special occasions or the self-playing digital pianos offering entertainment in shopping malls, restaurants, and airports.

One of the most profound developments in the history of musical instruments was the human harnessing of electricity. Early experiments in the electrification of metal strings date to mid-eighteenth-century France; the first electric instrument is considered the musical telegraph, patented by US inventor Elisha Gray in 1876. Some of the oldest electronic instruments—defined by their incorporation of circuitry and output of sound through loudspeakers—date to the early twentieth century. Many are now largely forgotten, including the telharmonium, introduced in the United States, the German Sphärophon, and the French ondes Martenot. One early electronic instrument that remains relatively popular is the theremin, invented in the Soviet Union in 1920. Distinctive both because of its operation, which requires the hands to move around two antennas without touching them, and its characteristic glissando—often described as "eerie" or otherworldly—the theremin became a staple of science fiction films starting in the 1950s and maintains a devoted following of practitioners and fans. The instrument was also featured in classical music recitals; performers such as Clara Rockmore and Lucie Bigelow Rosen became noted virtuosi in the United States.

An influential form of electronic music technologies is the synthesizer, a class of instruments that generate sound through a variety of analog and digital means. Synthesizers are commonly thought of as keyboard instruments, but early examples—such as the RCA Mark II or the Moog—were massive devices with rows of knobs and miles of cable, some of them resembling old-fashioned telephone switchboards. Synthesizers have been deployed by composers and performers of every stripe but came to be closely associated with Western pop music. Synthesizers became so influential in certain genres and subgenres that their sound nearly defines them, for example, the Moog and 1960s and 1970s

1. Lucie Bigelow Rosen plays a theremin in a 1936 recital. Her hands activate an electromagnetic field generated by the two antennas. Her right hand controls pitch (the closer the hand is to the vertical antenna, the higher the pitch), while her left controls volume (the closer to the horizontal loop antenna, the softer the sound).

psychedelic and progressive rock or the Yamaha DX7 and 1980s power ballads. Cousin to the synthesizer is the drum machine, an electronic instrument that generates percussive sounds and rhythmic patterns. Drum machines, too, have come to define the sound of popular music genres, including techno, electro, and hip hop. As novel, complex, and occasionally otherworldly as electronic instruments seem, there are more similarities than differences with their acoustic predecessors. Bongos and drum machines, harpsichords and digital keyboards are equally technologies of musical creation.

Notation and printing have been vital music technologies for centuries, allowing music to travel across space and time. Notation—the symbolic representation of musical performance—is the oldest technology used for musical recording and playback. It exists in diverse forms that come from cultures across the globe. The earliest discovered example of musical notation dates to about 1400 BCE, seen in a tablet found in Iraq (then Babylon) inscribed with cuneiform instructions for performing music on a lyre. For the twenty-eight centuries after this tablet was created, musical notation was only written by hand. Printed music appeared in the 1470s, some two decades after the advent of Johannes Gutenberg's printing press. The first substantial body of printed music, however, did not arrive until 1501, when Venetian printer Ottaviano Petrucci published *Harmonice musices odhecaton A*. Better known as the *Odhecaton*, it collected ninety-six compositions using moveable type, in which premade symbols are arranged to produce the desired text, with a series of three impressions—one for the staff, one for the notes, and the last for text. Successive innovations in printing led from moveable type to engraving to lithography. Even in the early twenty-first century, more than one hundred years after sound recording and radio made it possible to capture and disseminate musical performance in sonic form, notation and printing—now facilitated by specialized software—continue to serve the preservation and propagation of music.

Recording and radio are two technologies of sonic preservation and propagation that have loomed large in our musical lives for well over a century. The earliest known sound recording device was constructed by the French printer Édouard-Léon Scott de Martinville and patented in 1857. Although it may seem that any tool for preserving music should also be designed for playback, the machine, known as the phonautograph, was never intended to reproduce sounds; rather, Scott sought a way to analyze sound waves visually. Although the phonautograph never had a role in musical culture, the phonograph had an incalculable influence that continues to be felt. Yet when Thomas Edison and his team constructed the first working phonograph in December 1877—little more than a hand-cranked cylinder wrapped in tinfoil—its primary application was considered to be as a dictation device for businessmen. Music recordings started to proliferate in the 1890s, but it was not until famed opera singer Enrico Caruso started making records for the Victor Talking Machine Company in 1904 that the listening public took the technology seriously. (The terms phonograph, gramophone, talking machine, Victrola, and Graphophone, among others, while not technically synonymous, have come to be used almost interchangeably to refer to disc- or cylinder-equipped playback devices from the late nineteenth and early twentieth centuries.)

The history of sound recording includes key developments in modern music technology: 1877, the year Edison and his lab brought out the cylinder-playing phonograph; 1923, when microphones started replacing the megaphone-shaped acoustic recording horn; 1948, the birth year of the long-playing disc (LP) and the 45 rpm record; 1963, when the compact cassette tape went public; 1979, the debut of the Walkman; 1982, when the compact disc, or CD, was introduced; 1999, when Napster's peer-to-peer file-sharing service went live and MP3 became a household term; 2001, when the iPod, not the first but the most influential portable media player, hit the market; or 2008, which marked the launch of the music streaming service Spotify.

Radio—which disseminates sound via electromagnetic waves generated by transmitters, radiated across space through antennas, and collected by receivers—grew up alongside the phonograph. Italian inventor Guglielmo Marconi developed the first practical transmitters and receivers around 1895, and radio emerged as a commercial venture around 1900. Radio broadcasting, the transmission of audio content to the public, began around 1920, leading to the development of mass audiences for music programming. A radio receiver was first installed in an automobile in 1924 in Australia, creating a bond between music and cars that remains unbreakable. After the world started sinking into economic depression in 1929, it was said that radio, which provided free entertainment, would replace the phonograph, which required the purchase of records. But the two technologies came to coexist as radio programming increasingly moved from the broadcast of live musical performances to the playing of records. The intertwined histories of radio and recording can be seen, in microcosm, in the term commonly given to radio announcers whose programming features music: disc jockeys. Later milestones in the history of the technology include the introduction of the transistor radio in 1954, which greatly expanded the mobility of music, and Internet and satellite radio, coming out in 1993 and 1999, respectively, which allow music to be broadcast across a much wider geographical area than traditional, or what came to be called terrestrial, radio.

This summary is meant to provide context for discussions to come, but it requires a caveat. In recounting the triumphs of Petrucci, Marconi, and Edison we may promote what is known as the "great man theory," in which history is explained in terms of the impact of heroic, far-seeing men. Moreover, a narrow focus on objects and dates risks situating technology as the primary driver of musical experience and suggests that technology tends toward ever greater states of perfection. As useful as these chronicles are, we must understand that although names and dates matter to our understanding of music technology, culture matters most.

Culture matters

To see how culture matters to our understanding of music technology, consider the debates about Auto-Tune and the contested history of the harmonium in India. Not an instrument in itself, Auto-Tune is a pitch-correction software application. Debuting in 1997, it was designed as a behind-the-scenes tool to push a singer's wayward notes up or down subtly enough so listeners would not notice. Soon, however, it came to be used to create effects that the human voice could not otherwise achieve, and that were meant to be heard. When used in this way the voice moves from pitch to pitch with inhuman precision. Auto-Tune can also remove or regularize vibrato, the rapid wavering of pitch and intensity within a note that lends an emotional impact to a performance. Cher's 1998 "Believe" was the first hit song to employ Auto-Tune in such a conspicuous way, and its popularity encouraged others to adopt it as a musical feature and not simply as a corrective. R&B and hip hop artists embraced it wholeheartedly in the mid- and late-2000s; one of the most notable proponents was rapper T-Pain, who treated all his vocals with the software. Twenty years after its introduction, Auto-Tune was a fixture in recording studios worldwide, prominent in Algerian raï, Bollywood film songs from India, Japanese J-pop and Korean K-pop, South African kwaito, Tanzanian bongo flava, and Trinidadian soca.

Despite its popularity, Auto-Tune did not enjoy a seamless integration into existing musical practices. It initially provoked a vehement backlash: detractors called it gimmicky and lazy, describing the sound as inhuman, mechanical, or robotic. Defenders noted that Auto-Tune was hardly different from long-accepted technological interventions such as splicing (combining different parts or takes of a recording) and saw it as a means to express feelings, identities, and values through music more creatively and powerfully than would otherwise be possible.

The debates about Auto-Tune illustrate how technology reveals and refracts broader concerns and values. Within the African American gospel tradition, for example, both denunciations and defenses of Auto-Tune extend perennial debates about sacred music. Detractors say that Auto-Tune glorifies the singer rather than the Almighty; it makes a mockery of the idea of God-given talent when it is so clearly the product of human-made technology. Supporters contend that if Auto-Tuned gospel songs bring people into church and into God, they should be allowed to spread the Gospel and be celebrated for it. These arguments expose an old fault line within gospel—and many other forms of sacred music—between tradition and innovation, as well as the constant challenge faced by musicians who are called on to deploy their talents in the service of their deity without calling unseemly attention to their earthbound virtuosity.

The harmonium—a type of small pump organ and European import—became improbably popular across the Indian subcontinent in the twentieth century. Many Indian commentators saw this foreign music technology as a threat, describing it as a "plague," calling it the "bane of Indian music," or mocking it as the "harm-onium." All-India Radio refused to broadcast any music played on a harmonium for more than three decades. This contempt arose in part because its keyboard could not play all the notes in Indian scales and did not allow the smooth sliding between pitches characteristic of certain musical practices. The instrument also symbolized an unwelcome intrusion by the colonizing West, seen as an insidious attempt to pervert traditional practices and values.

Indian musicians and instrument makers, however, did not simply adopt the harmonium as they had found it. They adapted it to their traditions, practices, and aesthetics, for example, modifying the instrument so that it could be played sitting on the floor, as is traditional. Local culture was a decisive force in shaping the reception, adoption, and modification of the harmonium, as was

2. Vidyadhar Oke of Mumbai plays the harmonium in the customary Indian way, seated, with his right hand on the keyboard and his left operating the bellows. The instrument, which he designed, differs from the traditional European harmonium in that its keyboard has twenty-two notes per octave rather than twelve, allowing it to play scales used in Indian classical music.

the relationship between India and Europe, between the colonized and colonizer. Both music and technology are inevitably caught up in politics and power relations.

A twist in the story of the harmonium came when, in 2017, India's Goods and Services Tax Council decided to create a class of exemptions for a recently enacted nationwide 28 percent tax on musical instruments. The list of 134 exemptions was meant to encourage the purchase of indigenous instruments including such national symbols of India as the sitar and tabla. The harmonium also made it on the list. Why include an instrument of European origin with a Western keyboard on the list of "indigenous handmade musical instruments"? A clue comes in the way it is listed, as "Indian Harmonium." Having been adapted in appearance and performance practice over successive generations, it was seen as a distinct and indigenous instrument, an *Indian* harmonium that had come to reflect and represent the culture of its new home. In the relationship between music and technology, culture always matters.

The lure of technological determinism

To return to the opening story of resentful DJs in the digital age, the idea that music and musicians were better off "before technology took over" illustrates a problematic perspective known as technological determinism. This is the idea that the tools and systems that humans create have an outsized power to shape our actions and behavior and serve as a key force in social and historical change. John Philip Sousa articulated the concept in the first decade of the 1900s when he complained of the "menace of mechanical music." The player piano and phonograph, he claimed, would discourage amateur music making and generally "reduce the expression of music to a mathematical system of megaphones, wheels, cogs, disks, cylinders, and all manner of revolving things." In the twenty-first century, the algorithms that streaming platforms use to recommend songs to listeners are said to be "ruining music." These examples espouse a form of technological determinism, endowing technologies with agency and the power to influence our lives: they *take over* DJing, *reduce* the expression of music, or simply *ruin* it.

Deterministic language has an understandable appeal. It offers a simple explanation for complex phenomena and allows us to place responsibility for our actions on technology rather than on ourselves. Our short attention spans and our inclination to multitask, for example, seem connected to the proliferation of websites, television series, and computer applications. It is not *my* fault that I constantly check my smartphone and cannot focus on important tasks, like writing this book, when news and social media feeds beckon me. It is true that our interactions with technology are influenced and constrained by structures, conditions, and trends over which we have little control. But technological influence is more complex—and more interesting—than a simple deterministic view would lead us to believe. I might feel pressured to use a certain type of streaming service because I had become accustomed to an earlier version of it, or because the cost and trouble of switching would be considerable, or because not adopting it would exclude me from a musical community. Or I might feel distracted by the endless variety of informational technologies at my fingertips. But the constraint and proliferation of choice differ from the stark determinism of the view that "algorithms are ruining music."

Technological determinism does not necessarily encourage a pessimistic worldview. Often, and equally deterministically, technology is said to be the solution to the world's problems, great or small. For example, in the United States at the turn of the twentieth century, the phonograph was lauded as a cure for deafness, a way to calm "perturbed" patients during surgery, and the means to help America "become a more musical nation." At the turn of the twenty-first century, digital evangelists argued that peer-to-peer file-sharing and MP3s (typically in the form of the soon-to-be defunct Napster platform) portended the coming of the "celestial jukebox," a technology that would allow listeners to hear any music they might want whenever and wherever they desired, and at no cost.

Whether dystopian or utopian, determinist views of music technologies share the same problems. Both minimize the role of human agency and cultural forces. Instead of seeing ourselves as subject to the ineluctable power of technology, we should understand our relationship with technology as one shaped by our own will and creativity as well as by the broader contexts in which we live. The history of the accordion (a family of handheld instruments whose colloquial English name, squeezebox,

illustrates its operation) in the African island nation of
Madagascar offers an example. French settlers started bringing
accordions with them early in the period of colonial rule
(1897–1960), and Malagasy musicians came to adopt the
instrument as their own. Over time, as these instruments needed
repair, local accordionists altered its tuning, pushing back against
the Western scales embedded in the original design. They started
to play faster and more percussively than was usual among
European accordionists. In the West, these types of accordions
(which had two rows of buttons outlining a seven-note diatonic
scale) were largely regarded as simple folk instruments. In the
hands of Malagasy musicians, they could be instruments of
virtuosity. Moreover, they came to play a central role in sacred
rituals known as *tromba* that call the spirits of past royalty. The
accordion may have begun life in Madagascar as an import from a
distant metropole, but local musicians created new practices and
new meanings for the instrument. Responding to the design,
materiality, and affordances of the accordion and shaped by their
personal aesthetics as well as cultural values and historical
currents, artists adapted the instrument physically and
metaphorically. Although the accordion retained traces of its
French origins and heritage, it also became a vital symbol of
Malagasy spirituality and resistance.

Technology does not stand apart from music, influencing it from
the outside—it is a part of music, integral to every aspect of
musical activity and musical life. Technology has been central to
human music making at least since our Paleolithic ancestors
started making flutes. In fact, history has no record of a
pretechnological age of music. Humans are, and have always been,
creatures of technology and of music. If we want to understand
how music is made and experienced, if we want to know how
music travels and how it gains meaning, we must investigate its
relationship—ancient and inextricable—with technology.

Chapter 2
Bodies and senses

In 1924, the deafblind activist and author Helen Keller described a broadcast of Beethoven's Ninth Symphony, which she experienced by placing her hand on a radio's speaker: "What was my amazement to discover that I could feel, not only the vibrations, but also the impassioned rhythm, the throb and urge of the music! [. . .] When the human voices leaped up trilling from the surge of harmony, I recognized them instantly as voices. I felt the chorus grow more exultant, more ecstatic, *upcurving swift* and flame-like, until my heart almost stood still." When all the instruments and voices came together in the final movement, Keller described the feeling as "an ocean of heavenly vibration." It was not lost on her that when Beethoven composed this symphony he was, like her, deaf.

In 2017, scientist Lisa DeBruine posted a fanciful animation on social media of an anthropomorphic electrical tower jumping rope over a strand of wires held by two other towers. In the clip, the image vibrates when the tower hits the ground, suggesting an immense impact. Many viewers believe that they hear the tower land, DeBruine noted, even though no sound accompanies the video. Similar GIFs have demonstrated the same point, for example, an animation of two hands pounding a surface twice and then clapping. Many viewers of this silent clip attest to hearing the percussive opening of Queen's "We Will Rock You."

Hearing may be the primary sense through which most people receive music, but as these examples reveal, our other senses are vital as well. Helen Keller's experience of Beethoven on the radio may seem exceptional, but touch informs how people experience music all the time, even if they do not realize it. A simple way to feel music is to stand next to a large loudspeaker as it plays bass-heavy music; you will likely sense the music shaking the floor beneath your feet, rumbling in your chest cavity, even causing your hair or clothes to vibrate. The noisiness of the silent animations points to another phenomenon, known as *visually evoked auditory response*, also referred to as *vearing*, to suggest the act of hearing with one's eyes. Vearing occurs when visual stimuli induce auditory sensations. This can happen through association; we know the sound of hands clapping so we sense that sound even when we only see the motion. But some people hear with their eyes even when there is no such association. Such sensory crosstalk is called synesthesia—a small number of people have vivid experiences of colors or flavors when they hear certain sounds or words, for example. But there is a more common phenomenon at play here: our senses engage with each other, and the boundaries between them are not as clear as we assume.

Our bodies are the primary and constant mediators of the music we experience. Even if we are alone, singing to ourselves, we experience mediated music. Flesh, bone, and air cavities shape our song as it travels through our bodies and to our ears and is interpreted by our brain's auditory cortex. This is in part why we sound different to ourselves when we hear our recorded voices: we no longer experience our voices from the inside out. Recording devices mediate our voices differently from the way our bodies do when we create the sound ourselves. More broadly speaking, technology mediates the relationship between music and the human body. Often technologies offer a compromise: in providing new ways to experience music, they limit access to some of our senses. Most typically, sight is compromised. Radio, recordings, and streaming audio expand musical access to our ears while limiting access to our eyes. And yet, the removal of one sensory channel can provide new ways to experience music; in some cases, the invisibility of a music's physical source can heighten its impact.

Unseen music

Across cultures and time, music made in places of worship has sometimes been meant to be heard but *not* seen. Bells, for example, tap the power of unseen music, summoning worshippers and marking time and sacred occasions. They toll throughout the world, whether each morning and night from Buddhist temples or on Sundays and during funerals for Christians. In Russian Orthodox Christianity, the instruments are themselves sacred, and new bells are blessed in a ritual akin to a baptism. Unseen, sacred sounds are manifested in other ways as well. Muslim chanters, or *muezzins*, call the devoted five times a day, now often amplified by loudspeakers, from on high in mosque minarets. Ponderous chords thunder from musicians hidden in the organ lofts of many Christian churches.

Although disembodied music may evoke a sense of awe or foster a feeling of connection with the infinite, it can also be disconcerting. In the early twentieth century, when the phonograph and radio were still new, bodiless music generated cognitive dissonance in some listeners. The illustrated song phonograph, popular in public venues in the United States, offered one way to resolve this dissonance. The machine displayed photographs of musicians or painted nature scenes as records played so as to reunite the senses. On early radio programs, musicians and announcers invoked the sense of sight in their banter, helping audiences conjure images of performers as well as fellow listeners. The radio industry also published magazines and songbooks to give listeners something to look at (and something to buy). In a 1932 songbook US radio entertainer Bradley Kincaid appealed to sight as well as touch in addressing his fans: "When I sing for you on the air, I always visualize you, a family group, sitting around the radio, listening and commenting on my program. If I did not feel your presence, though you be a thousand miles away, the radio would be cold and unresponsive to me, and I in turn would sound the same way to you. Sometimes I feel that I could almost reach out and shake your hand and give you a cheery 'good morning,' and I wish I could." Los Angeles DJ Al Jarvis encouraged home listeners to imagine being in the presence of the great jazz bands of the 1930s. Calling his program a "make-believe ballroom," he sought to "create in the minds of the dialers that they are skimming across the dance floor." It was such a popular gambit that other DJs soon followed suit.

Over the years, strategies for compensating for the missing senses were deployed less and less, both as consumers accepted the invisibility of the musicians they heard and as sound film, which reunited the aural and visual experience of music, became viable and popular. In the mid-twentieth century, some musicians worked explicitly to develop a practice of unseen music. French composer Pierre Schaeffer used the word *acousmatic* to identify sound that one hears without seeing the causes behind it. The word derives from the ancient Greek *akousmatikoi*—literally "those who hear"—the name given to disciples of the philosopher Pythagoras, who listened to their teacher's lectures behind a veil or curtain without being able to see his physical form. For Schaeffer and other experimental composers, the separation of sound from its physical source was something not to be avoided but explored. Scores of composers exploited the possibilities of phonographs, tape players, and loudspeakers to create music that challenged the traditional connection between sight and sound.

Feeling sound: musical haptics

The English percussion virtuoso Evelyn Glennie gets annoyed when people constantly ask how she can be a musician who is profoundly deaf. Her response is that she hears music by sensing and interpreting sonic vibrations, which is what every musician does. All music consists of vibrations, disturbances in air molecules that are converted into electrical signals and then interpreted as sound. Hearing people experience these vibrations through their ears and tend not to interpret such sensations as tactile. But Glennie does, and she has attuned her body to determine the relative pitch of sounds based on where she feels their vibrations: lower pitches in her feet and legs, higher ones in her face, neck, or chest. This is how Glennie hears. "Hearing," she explains, "is basically a specialized form of touch."

Glennie also hears by directly touching her instruments; she knows what kinds of sounds they are producing by how they feel as they are being played. This is known as vibrotactile feedback—information received through the vibrations we sense when touching an object. If you have a mobile phone in your pocket and feel it vibrate, the type, length, and repetition of the vibration tell you that you are receiving a call or some kind of message or alert. Video game controllers employ this type of feedback as well, with rumbles and shudders often as instructive as anything that might appear on the screen. Helen Keller used vibrotactile feedback to experience Beethoven when she put her hands on a radio speaker while his music played. Vibrotactile feedback is just one of the ways in which we receive information through touch, and there is a broader term that encompasses this form of communication: haptics. Haptic communication includes not just vibration, but also texture, pressure, and temperature.

Haptic communication is increasingly incorporated into the world of music technology. Some digital musical instruments can emulate the kind of tactile feedback musicians receive when playing acoustic instruments, such as the resistance a traditional piano key provides when pressed, a sensation pianists often refer to as "touch." But haptics can do more than simulate traditional instruments and can enliven wholly new musical devices and provide novel forms of feedback—for example, controllers with touchscreens that provide tactile sensations, even cold or heat, to differentiate among sounds and musical techniques.

And then there are the wearables. These can be worn as clothes or accessories or affixed to the body. Some are designed for performers, some for listeners, some for both. Why don a haptic belt or glove, armband, or vest? It can compensate for something that is missing, for example, by imparting the sense of deep, rumbling bass without the need for massive speakers. Wearables can be used to enhance musical experience by providing new forms of vibrotactile feedback, encouraging a stronger sense of musical immediacy or connection with a performer. It could pulse in time with a performer's vibrato or rhythmic gestures, allowing the listener to feel the music more intimately, perhaps even fostering a sense of participation in the music making. Wearables can enable listeners to focus on different parts of an ensemble, heightening, say, the prominence of the brass in one passage and percussion in another. We might call these experiences a kind of augmented musical reality. Experiments have also explored the use of haptics as a form of communication among performers, enabling them to provide cues to adjust musical parameters— tempo, volume, rhythm, and so on—in ways that might be difficult to convey through their voices or gestures.

Researchers are still trying to understand why some forms of haptic feedback enhance musical engagement and others do not and why some listeners report that the wearables soothe them or make them want to dance while others complain that they are distracting, uncomfortable, even physically violating. Although wearables have yet to become widely adopted among concertgoers, haptic vests, belts, or armbands may one day regularly accompany us into dance clubs and concert venues. If haptic music technology is broadly accepted, it will not be because of its novelty, however, but rather because it lets us feel music in ever more powerful, meaningful ways.

Androids, Vocaloids, and holograms: old and new forms of musical embodiment

Phonographs and player pianos were not the first technologies to separate musical sound from the bodies that created them. Bodiless music making existed for more than two millennia in the form of self-playing musical instruments such as music boxes and water-powered organs. Sometimes, however, inventors and artists sought to endow these automata with bodies. Although largely forgotten now, music-making androids performed for audiences across Europe and the United States through much of the eighteenth and nineteenth centuries. (Though it sounds futuristic, *android* is an old word, appearing as early as 1728 to describe a humanlike automaton.) In 1738, Jacques de Vaucanson exhibited two life-sized instrument-playing male androids to much fanfare in Paris, while in 1774, the Swiss Jaquet-Droz family produced a harpsichord-playing female android with a five-song repertoire. Dutch inventor Cornelius van Oecklen took an "android clarinetist"—whose guts included clockwork motors, bellows, springs, and a pinned barrel (like that of a music box)—on tours of the Netherlands in the 1830s and the United States in 1856 and 1861. Concert reviews noted that it performed competently and moved its arms, head, and eyes as it played. Spectators were allowed to look inside the android, slightly larger than an average person, to see that there was no "humbug." The word *curious* comes up again and again in these reviews. These curious androids were hardly mainstream technologies, but they illustrate the centuries-long anxiety and wonder that the separation of music from the human body has provoked. These often quite realistic-looking figures occupied what later came to be known as the uncanny valley, a phenomenon in which human replicas elicit a mixture of attraction and revulsion.

More than 250 years after Vaucanson's android came the Vocaloid system, a software application whose name is a portmanteau of *vocal* and *android*. Released by the Japanese manufacturer

3. This automaton was built by the Swiss watchmaker Henri-Louis Jaquet-Droz in 1774. The female figure operates a small organ through articulated fingers that depress the keys; her eyes, head, and chest move as well, mimicking the gestures of a human performer. These movements are created by a complex mechanism of metal levers, barrels, cylinders, and cams.

Yamaha in 2004, it allows users to compose songs by drawing on banks of professionally recorded vocal samples, just as one might use a traditional digital audio workstation or DAW—a software platform for recording, editing, and producing audio files—to create musical tracks out of libraries of instrumental sounds. The voices are human, but the songs, assembled out of individually sung words whose sonic parameters (pitch, duration, timbre, etc.) are readily manipulated, exist only in the digital realm, never having been performed by an actual singer. Vocaloid-composed songs thus live in the uncanny valley—humanoid, but not quite human.

Vocaloid songs are disembodied, but it was not long after the introduction of the technology that digital avatars, often in the form of anime characters, were introduced to "perform" their music. Hatsune Miku, a turquoise-pigtailed teenage Vocaloid girl, was released (or "born," according to her creator, Crypton Future Media) in 2007. Her name means "the first sound from the future," and like the androids of the past she seems to dwell in the realm of science fiction. Hatsune Miku is just one many Vocaloid characters, and hundreds of thousands of songs have been composed for these personas. Fans are encouraged to create music for them as well as to develop variations on their visual image. This crowdsourcing strategy, drawing on what is known as user-generated content, fosters fierce dedication and has contributed to their continuing popularity. Vocaloid avatars first took root in Japan but have become popular—and are taken very seriously—around the world. The Chinese Vocaloid idol, Luo Tianyi (like Miku, an energetic teenaged girl), became a beloved cultural figure, not only spawning a large repertoire of pop songs but also serving as a celebrity endorser for top-selling brands and performing duets with classical pianist and countryman Lang Lang. In 2013, Hatsune Miku starred in the first Vocaloid opera, with costumes by US fashion designer Marc Jacobs, creative director of the French fashion house Louis Vuitton. Titled *The End*, it offers a meditation on mortality, voiced by a human creation that complicates our understanding of life, death, and existence.

Hatsune Miku first existed as a bank of vocal sounds, then as a collection of songs, and then as a two-dimensional figure. In 2009 she gained a dimension, or at least the appearance of it, and became a hologram. In the following years she toured the world, with glowstick-waving crowds singing along as her life-sized image fronted a band of living musicians. She was not actually a hologram, nor are any of the dozens of video likenesses of musicians—from classical artists Maria Callas and Glenn Gould to rapper Tupac Shakur and the composer and performer Frank Zappa—that have been billed as holograms. A hologram is a form of three-dimensional photography that captures and projects the contours of a solid surface. The reason actual holograms are rare is that they require powerful lasers that pose a danger to anyone who comes in contact with them; moreover, they capture still images and not movement, making them useless for recreating live performance. The "holograms" that are billed as such in the early twenty-first century are two-dimensional video images projected onto transparent scrims or glass panes that only suggest a freedom of movement. These video projections descend from a technology developed by English scientist John Pepper in 1862, who created a similar effect—which came to be called Pepper's ghost—using a bright light and a pane of glass to give the illusion of an otherworldly figure moving about a stage.

But because of Princess Leia, these video images are commonly referred to as holograms. A long time ago in a galaxy far, far away, a droid known as R2-D2 projected a three-dimensional likeness of a princess in distress. As depicted in the 1977 film *Stars Wars*, the hologram sparked the imaginations of millions, including those who would go on to create simulacra of beloved musical figures. Within the world of *Star Wars*, the reason to have a hologram, as opposed to a text or recorded message, was to impart what other forms of communication could not—a sense of physical presence as a well as the immediacy and urgency that posture, facial expressions, and gestures can convey. These are some of the reasons that musicians have been recreated in hologram form.

Perhaps the best-known example of a hologrammed musician was rapper Tupac Shakur. Murdered in 1996, his image was recreated for a performance with fellow hip hop artists Dr. Dre and Snoop Dog at the 2012 Coachella festival in California. The performance was a surprise. The crowd of 80,000 watched in disbelief as the dead rapper appeared onstage and proceeded to greet his old friends and call out to the crowd. He performed "Hail Mary," a posthumously released song that opens with a spoken-word introduction that includes these biblically inspired lines: "And God said he should send his one begotten son / To lead the wild into the ways of the man / Follow me, eat my flesh, flesh of my flesh." He later raps, "I'm a ghost in these killing fields." The themes of resurrection and the otherworldly were impossible to miss. Shakur's digital resurrection was complicated and expensive, requiring a team of animators and engineers six weeks, at a cost of $600,000, to perform two songs. The project also enlisted a body double who was filmed imitating the rapper's movements onstage and a video of the artist's head manipulated through computer-generated images, necessary because Shakur was never filmed performing the song. One of the ironies of the modern musical hologram trend is that for every incorporeal performer, many more flesh-and-bone humans are required, whether behind the scenes as technicians or body doubles or onstage as backing bands or co-performers. It is very much a hybrid of the virtual and the real.

Why raise dead musicians as holograms? Given that these artists have left rich legacies of recorded sound, what is the appeal of their physical, bodily presence even if it is clearly an illusion? A variety of impulses are at play. In a way, musical holograms are like tribute bands, which offer fans something that recordings of the actual artists cannot: a sense of the spectacle, spontaneity, and interactivity of live performances, the ritual and communal ethos of concerts. Seeing the artists' bodies moving onstage can foster a powerful form of connection, even communion, with a beloved figure, one that may take on a spiritual dimension for devotees. For those who had seen live performances of those musicians, holograms can arouse powerful memories; for those who had never had the opportunity to be in the physical presence of their favorite performers, a hologram might be the next best thing.

Holograms are not just for the dead. Living artists, too, have found reason to record holograms, among them Korean artists and bands within the globally popular phenomenon known as K-pop. The process for live artists is intensive, requiring them to be filmed with motion-capture suits, full-body outfits with embedded sensors that take physical measurements and record the wearer's movements. Though more difficult and time-consuming than creating a typical music video, it allows for new movements and gestures to be created once all the data are recorded. For the K-pop stars who have been hologrammed, the investment allows them (or their likenesses) to perform when and where they cannot and do so without the fatigue and risk that live performances demand of them. It is a way of transforming an ephemeral phenomenon into a reproducible and ideally very lucrative commodity.

In 2013 and 2014, two dazzling theaters, K-live and SMTOWN, were built in Seoul, South Korea, specifically to cater to the legions of K-pop fans. In both cases, the holograms were part of a hybrid form of entertainment that combined the virtual and the real. Live dancers and other entertainers engaged with crowds before and during the hologram performances. Visitors enjoyed a more interactive experience than they would have otherwise—patrons were encouraged to "touch your favorite stars." Lucky fans were filmed ahead of the show and then projected on video screens to give the illusion that they were singing or dancing with the biggest K-pop acts.

In the early years of the 2010s, holograms made headlines and drew large crowds around the world. By the end of the decade, however, they had not fulfilled the potential predicted for them. Demand waned; concertgoers reported disappointment. The hologram phenomenon did not quite die, but these musical phantasms never quite lived, either. Perhaps that was the problem.

Disembodied music and sightless listening have provoked consternation and awe over the millennia. The interventions may be intentional, as when musicians and instruments are hidden from sight. Or the effect can be the byproduct of the technology, as with recorded, broadcast, or streamed music. The responses that these technologies arouse are fascinating and varied. Sometimes the goal is to restore what is missing, whether by building androids or programming Vocaloids, painting slides for illustrated song phonographs, or updating a Victorian magic trick in the form of simulated holograms. We can also embrace bodiless, invisible music to focus our listening and to forge a connection with the immaterial or spiritual world. All these examples, however, serve to demonstrate a simple but underappreciated fact: that we experience music with our whole bodies, our whole beings.

Chapter 3
Time

What can transport us to the past? Propel us into the future?
Slow time to a crawl and accelerate it to breakneck speeds?
What can fold time in on itself, replaying the same moment over
and over again? The answer is music. A childhood song conjures
memories so vivid that decades fall away in an instant. Music
absorbs our attention, contracting and dilating time: a three-
minute song stretches languidly; a quarter-hour piece passes in
a flash. Through the repetition of short passages or the
sounding of unchanging pitches, music can even make time
seem to stop.

Witnessing the cycles of days, months, seasons, and years, humans
have always marveled at time's inexorability. Time can be a
blessing, a healer, a giver of wisdom. Time, which no one outlives,
can also inspire dread. Our fascination with time has led us to
develop tools for marking and tracking it, from sundials and
calendars to wristwatches and atomic clocks. Music is also such a
tool, a time machine that shapes our experience of every passing
moment. It makes sense, then, that so many of the technologies of
musical creation, preservation, and dissemination—whether
notation and the metronome or tape loops and digital
quantization—were created expressly to enhance music's ability to
shape time.

Ordering time

Whether it slips away from us or we lose track of it, time is elusive, unruly. Still, we do our best to impose order on it, and over the ages we have developed a host of musical tools for that purpose. One of the earliest is notation, a technology for preserving and disseminating music that dates back at least 2,400 years. Consider conventional Western notation. The black and white ovals, some with stems and some without, affix the duration of notes; the vertical bar lines that divide the horizontal lines of the staff corral these notes into orderly collections called measures; curved lines above or below a series of notes gather them into distinctive phrases; a thick double vertical line with two dots next to it requires a section of music to be repeated. Each tradition of music notation has its distinctive symbols and instructions for keeping time and its own approach to prescribing or describing sounds. For example, *Gongche*, a notational system developed during China's Tang dynasty (618–907 CE), uses Chinese characters to represent notes and smaller symbols to indicate strong and weak beats, but duration and rhythm are not specified. These are left to tradition and the discretion of musicians.

A newer, but still centuries-old technology that tracks time is the metronome. The word comes from an 1815 patent written by German inventor Johann Nepomuk Mälzel for an automatic pendulum designed to emit a ticking sound at precise intervals. Mälzel stands accused of incorporating much of the work of Dutchman Dietrich Nikolaus Winkel, who had proposed a similar chronometer the previous year. Unfortunately for Winkel, it is Mälzel's name that has been immortalized in Western music history. The common abbreviation for tempo in European classical music, M.M. (as in M.M. = 120, or 120 beats per minute), is short for "Mälzel's metronome." The device attracted the attention of Ludwig van Beethoven, who had first approached Mälzel to build him an early type of hearing aid known as an ear trumpet. Beethoven became convinced that the metronome would be an indispensable tool for indicating the precise tempos of his own works and thus ensuring (he hoped, but in vain) that musicians would play his music exactly as he instructed. Although Beethoven was both specific and adamant about the strict adherence to the numerical tempo markings he assigned to his music, a two-century-long debate has ensued about the appropriateness and feasibility of honoring his wishes. On the one hand, the markings supply valuable information about how Beethoven wished his music to be executed, and some insist that performers are obligated to honor these wishes, or at least try. Others argue that musicians must be allowed the freedom to perform Beethoven as they see fit; moreover, many of his pieces are considered unplayable at his desired tempos.

A twentieth-century descendant of the metronome was the click track, originally created as a tool for synchronizing music to film. At first it was a strip of film onto which the recurring click of a metronome was recorded. Film musicians would play in tempo with the click track, which was played over their headphones but was not recorded onto the final soundtrack. The steady, uniform tempo of the music made it easier to coordinate sound and image. We have Mickey Mouse largely to thank—or blame—for the click track. In 1931, the Walt Disney Company filed a patent for a "method and apparatus for synchronizing photoplays," which includes three cartoon drawings of Mickey sitting at a piano and playing a chord. As the accompanying text explains, the challenge is to coordinate precisely the procession of drawings—which fly by at a rate of twenty-four per frames per second—with the sounds meant to accompany them.

Ironically, although the patent (granted in 1933) was invaluable to Walt Disney, one of the first animated films the company produced afterward depicts a metronome as a literal prison. The 1935 short film, *Music Land*, tells of two star-crossed musical instruments, a violin from the Land of Symphony and a saxophone from its enemy, the Isle of Jazz. When the sax crosses

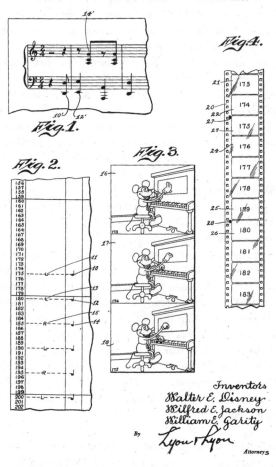

4. The first page of the 1931 Disney patent, "Method and Apparatus for Synchronizing Photoplays." Fig. 1 is a fragment of a song that would be played by Mickey Mouse (whose motions are shown in Fig. 3). Fig. 2 is part of a synchronization sheet showing a sequence of frames (indicated by the numbers on the left) and the particular notes played by the left (L) or right (R) hand; Fig. 4 shows a strip of film with the numbers indicating frames and notes.

5. Composer Daphne Oram draws on 35mm film strips using a device she created called the Oramics machine, which consisted of photoelectric cells that converted the black ink lines into music.

the Sea of Discord to meet his beloved, he is captured and locked inside a large, wind-up pendulum metronome. The metronome cannot contain the exuberant independence of jazz, however, and the horn escapes, reuniting with his stringed love. The click track came to have a prominent place in both animated and live-action film, and its influence remains strong in the twenty-first century. Musicians in pop groups, who often record their parts separately, use click tracks to establish consistent tempos that allow different takes of the recording to be combined into a coherent final product. Some musical groups—for example, theater orchestras and church ensembles—use click tracks during live performances when it may be difficult to hear fellow musicians or see a conductor or director.

For generations, musicians have performed with metronomes and the like steadily clicking in the background, whether individually to master difficult passages or in groups to create consensus among musicians. Although few people profess love for it, the metronome is widely considered a valuable tool. But many rail against it, decrying it as annoying, dehumanizing, oppressive, or unmusical. Disney's *Music Land*, which both depended on and condemned the metronome, captures this ambivalence. Less ambivalent were two twentieth-century works, Japanese composer Toshi Ishiyanagi's *Music for Electric Metronomes* (1960) and *Poème symphonique* (1962), a work for 100 metronomes by Hungarian György Ligeti. The "proper" use of a metronome demands that they be operated singly, that they support musicians but are never heard by audiences. These pieces, however, call for metronomes without musicians, multitudes of them unleashing a chaotic soundscape that undermines the device's disciplinarian function.

Notation and the metronome are tools that guide the timing of performers. A more recent development, quantization, acts directly on recorded sound. Quantization is the process of regularizing rhythmic inconsistencies in a digital sound file. Imagine singing or playing music with a metronome. No matter how precise you try to be, you will never be perfectly synchronized with each beat. If you were to capture that snippet using a digital audio workstation (or DAW) you could see just how far you are from a steady beat. If you are not as close as you would like, you can use the quantize function to snap those wayward rhythms into place.

Quantization is an essential feature of modern sound recording. But precision and consistency are relative goods, and too much can sap music of its vitality. Sometimes composers, engineers, and producers seek the opposite of quantization. This is typically the case with music composed using musical instrument digital interface (MIDI), a technology widely used to create and manipulate electronic music. Music created with MIDI starts out inhumanly precise. Most digital audio workstations now have a function designed to counteract the effect of relentless precision and consistency. This is the so-called humanize function. It allows for a randomization of different parameters of the music, slightly changing a note's length, position, or emphasis. This function can be applied automatically without the need to nudge individual notes; just set certain parameters and let the software do the rest. The humanize function is now such a staple of recording and composing sessions on DAWs that there seems to be no irony intended in the video tutorials that promise to teach viewers "how to automatically humanize" MIDI-made music. Yes, a great deal of computer code has been written to automate the process of making music sound more human.

The popularity of the humanize function reveals the ambivalence artists feel about the tools they use to shape musical time. On the one hand, these technologies serve a desire for consistency and unity, stability and translatability; they make it possible to preserve the musical intentions of composers, to align and unify performers, to bring sound and sight together, and to achieve an aesthetically pleasing level of musical precision (or imprecision). On the other hand, these tools have raised serious concerns about the loss of musical individuality and freedom and the homogenization of practices and styles. A 2017 study observed a remarkable change in the consistency of tempos in Western pop music between 1955 and 2014. Examining tempo variation in nearly 1,100 pop songs over the sixty-year period, it showed that between 1955 and 1959 the average standard deviation of tempo in these songs was five beats per minute (about 4.8 percent), a noticeable amount of variation. Between 2010 and 2014, however, pop songs in this period were significantly more consistent, varying less than one beat per minute, or 0.85 percent, of the average tempo. Why the change? The authors point to the introduction and widespread use of electronic drum machines, click tracks, MIDI, and quantization, all tools used to create temporal consistency in music. Whether this consistency is considered a good or a bad thing is a subjective assessment, but there is no doubt that our use of these tools has unmistakably shaped how we make and experience music.

Limiting time

Since the late 1800s, musicians and listeners have been grappling with the limited capacity of recording media. Most wax cylinders, the first commercial format, held between about two and four minutes of music; shellac 78 rpm discs, most typically ten or twelve inches in diameter, preserved around three to five minutes per side; the seven-inch 45 rpm record and the twelve-inch 33⅓ rpm record, both vinyl formats introduced in the late 1940s, captured between three to five and sixteen to twenty-five minutes per side, respectively (rpm stands for revolutions per minute, the standard unit of speed for flat discs). Magnetic tape, which first came spooled on reels, varied widely in its capacity—from a few minutes to a few hours—depending on the size of the reel and the length of the tape. Compact cassette tapes, introduced in the early 1960s, were more standardized, usually with lengths of thirty, sixty, or ninety minutes.

In the several decades before the introduction of 33⅓ rpm discs—called LPs because they were "long playing"—composers who wanted to record their music often had to do one of two things: cut or expand existing pieces to fit the medium or create new works with the time limitations in mind. (Performers could also play a piece faster than normal to shave seconds off its time, but this was rarer.) Some of the most prominent Western classical composers of the twentieth century—among them Edward Elgar, Gabriel Fauré, Paul Hindemith, Igor Stravinsky, and Kurt Weill—wrote pieces specifically so they could fit on one side of a 78 rpm record. The US composer Roy Harris cheekily called his made-to-order 1934 chamber work for flute and strings *Four Minutes-20 Seconds*.

Improvising musicians, particularly working in the early years of recording, had an even more acute challenge. First, they had to plan the length and structure of the music *before* the performance. (In live settings these decisions could be made in the moment depending on the will of the performers and the enthusiasm of the audience.) And then they had to execute precisely timed performances. Running even a few seconds long could ruin a take, a costly expenditure of time, energy, and money. Sitarist Ravi Shankar described the need to adjust the length of his improvised ragas (pieces based on melodic modes in Indian classical music) as a form of "mental discipline":

> Suppose I know that I have to play for a little record of 78 speed, that means 3 minutes, only. I know that I have to play for a long-playing record, that means anything between 18 to 20 or 21 minutes. I know I have to play for a [radio or TV] broadcast of half an hour. Or I know that I have to play [a live concert] in India, for instance, I'm supposed to play at least for 2 hours one item, one raga. So you see, I have to immediately conceive that this is the period in which I have to play the raga.

Such extreme variation in the length of pieces is hardly uncommon: musicians improvising around the Arabic *maqam*, the twelve-bar blues of American jazz, the *dastgāh* of Iranian art music, and countless other traditions must learn how to tailor the length of their performances to the requirements of different media. The legacy of these technologically imposed restrictions persists into the twenty-first century. It is no coincidence that pop songs of many different traditions still run three to four minutes long, the length of ten-inch 78 rpm shellac discs and the vinyl 45 rpm.

As much as composers and performers faced the challenges of working within the temporal limitations of sound recording, by far the largest affected group was the worldwide audience of listeners. For nearly a century, from the time of the earliest commercial recordings in the 1890s until the widespread adoption of the compact disc in the 1980s, millions of listeners performed a repeated set of movements at regular intervals, picking up the record player's tone arm, gently turning the record over (or replacing it with a new one), and then carefully placing the needle in the correct groove to start the next side or disc. Speaking of the era of wind-up phonographs and 78 rpm records, US blues musician Son House recalled the trials of "gettin' up, settin' it back, turnin' it around, crankin' the crank, primin' it up, and lettin' the horn down again," and doing this every three or four minutes. More recently, I asked my father on his seventy-eighth birthday whether he was nostalgic for the days when he listened to records. "I have no interest in listening to vinyl records," he told me. "Why?" I asked. "Because I *remember* them," he explained. "What a pain in the ass they were. I'd rather listen to a CD." Of the many ways that the mediation of music through sound recordings has manifested itself, it is perhaps the generations-long time limitation that has most frequently, noticeably, and intrusively affected the listening experience.

Stretching time, accelerating time

What do Ludwig van Beethoven and Justin Bieber have in common? Rather little, except that other musicians have utterly transformed the sound and sense of their music by radically slowing it. In 2002, Oslo-based composer Leif Inge slowed a recording of Beethoven's Ninth Symphony so that the normally seventy-minute piece became twenty-four hours long. He called this version "9 Beet Stretch"; it sounds so drastically different from the original that perhaps it is better understood as a wholly new work. In 2010, Florida producer Nick Pittsinger created a thirty-five-minute opus by slowing Bieber's "U Smile" by 800 percent, altering the lilting mid-tempo love song into an ethereal, languid soundscape. Both Inge and Pittsinger used a digital technique known as time stretching, in which the speed or duration of an audio signal (such as a recording of music) can be changed without affecting the pitch.

Several decades earlier, US-born musicians Conlon Nancarrow and Ross Bagdasarian experimented with accelerating musical sounds beyond what was typically considered normal, even humanly possible. Between the 1930s and 1990s, Nancarrow used a mechanical player piano to compose and reproduce works so complex, rhythmically precise, and fast that human pianists cannot perform most of them. In 1958, Ross Bagdasarian started creating music for a virtual band he called Alvin and the Chipmunks by recording his voice on a reel-to-reel tape machine at half speed and then playing it back at full speed. Accelerating and multiplying his voice, the result was a group of high-pitched, squeaky singers that suggested what a group of striped rodents might sound like if they could sing. (In this predigital age, it was not possible to decouple speed and pitch; thus, the faster the recording, the higher the pitch.) Bagdasarian was not the first to experiment in this way—he had been inspired by the distinctive vocal sound of the Munchkins in the 1939 film *The Wizard of Oz*, which was created with similar techniques.

These cases demonstrate a long and ongoing fascination with the technological acceleration and deceleration of music. Some of the examples were one-off experiments; others led to larger bodies of works. There are whole genres based on and named for their relative tempos, for example, slowcore and speedcore, subgenres that emerged in the 1990s that also depend on music technologies for their existence. In the twenty-first century, users of the video-sharing platforms YouTube and TikTok have posted countless fast and slow versions of pop songs, often under the categories of nightcore (named after the Norwegian duo Nightcore, which gained fame through its accelerated remixes) and, on the other end of the speed spectrum, slowed + reverb.

Two late twentieth-century genres, one slow and one fast, illuminate the entanglements of technology and culture in the exploration of musical speed. Chopped and screwed (a clear predecessor to slowed + reverb) is a form of hip hop that rose to prominence in the southern US city of Houston in the early 1990s. The name comes in part from DJ Screw, who introduced the genre. His innovation was to use the pitch adjust control on the analog turntable against its intended use. The pitch adjust is typically a slider that allows DJs to make subtle alterations in the speed of a rotating disc. Changing the speed of a record affects its pitch, raising or lowering it depending on whether it is accelerated or slowed. The control is typically used to create smooth, barely noticeable transitions between songs by aligning the tempos of successive tracks through slight adjustments. DJ Screw shone the sonic equivalent of a spotlight on this control, drastically slowing rapped vocals from 90–100 beats per minute (bpm) to 60–70 bpm, which pushed them down into a baritone or bass range. (He also employed tape recorders to help achieve this effect.) In addition to slowing the music, DJ Screw "chopped" sounds, fragmenting and repeating them so as to draw attention to certain phrases. The effect is striking, imparting a languorous feel and hypnotic sensibility to the sound.

Chopped and screwed music did not simply reflect the aesthetics of its creator. Its tempo also reflected the slower pace of life in the US South and the aesthetics of a segment of Black, urban youth in Houston. Its laidback, woozy vibe resonated with and facilitated activities enjoyed by those who listened to this music: cruising in cars rather than racing them; relaxing while listening to music rather than dancing to it; and consuming substances to mellow one's mood, such as alcohol, marijuana, and, most famously, "purple drank," a mix of prescription cough syrup and soda. Whether intentionally or not, this music and lifestyle also represents a form of resistance to cultural norms that prioritize speed in all aspects of life. Chopped and screwed music can be seen as part of a global "slow movement": it resists sensory overload; it promotes relaxation over hyperactivity; it opposes the homogenization of modern capitalist culture by focusing on the hyperlocal. Despite its distinctly regional roots, however, the sound of chopped and screwed has come to have a global influence, suggesting that its exploitation of music technologies to reflect the values of slowness resonates well beyond Houston.

Like chopped and screwed, drum and bass is a genre that arose out of a Black urban musical community in the early 1990s. However, it is not just an ocean that separates them—drum and bass arose in London—but also about 100 beats per minute, with most tracks clocking in between 160 and 180 bpm. The spare, reverb-laden sound of drum and bass points to the influence of reggae and dub and the Caribbean roots of early practitioners, but its most notable attribute is its sheer London-born speed. Drum and bass tracks are largely instrumental (though they often feature brief, repeating vocal samples), typically built around a short percussion solo digitally sampled from an older funk, soul, or rock record. By far the most frequently and famously sampled song in drum and bass is "Amen Brother" (1969) by the US group the Winstons, specifically a four-bar, seven-second slice of syncopated funk that appears a bit after the halfway point. The break is already fast, at about 135 bpm, but early drum and bass DJs used the turntable's controls to alter the speed of the original, first by changing the default record speed from 33⅓ to 45 rpm and then pushing the pitch adjust to its highest setting. (Some DJs hacked their turntables to double the amount by which they could adjust tempo.) Drum and bass reflects the culture of acceleration of its early years, a time when the Internet was emerging as a global force and the rapidly increasing flow of information was experienced as simultaneously exhilarating, frenetic, and overwhelming. The ways in which people often dance to drum and bass literally embody the genre's complex response to acceleration. Some use slow, controlled movements evoking the graceful, deliberate motions of Chinese tai chi and Brazilian capoeira in a style often described as liquid dancing. Another dance style, x-outing, features more percussive footwork in which heel and toe taps alternate in rapid succession.

What is crucial to the aesthetics and meaning of chopped and screwed and drum and bass is not so much that they are slow and fast, but also that they sound distinctly *slowed down* and *sped up*.

This artistic deceleration and acceleration sonically symbolize the agency of the musicians. It is not incidental that these genres emerged from communities that had long faced racial discrimination, economic hardship, and limited access to technology; the musicians are part of a capitalist system that values innovation, technological knowhow, and hustle, but they rarely profit from their ingenuity and creativity. How these genres engage with speed reveals the complex ways that their communities interact with and view the world around them. By embracing sounds that could only be created, at least at first, by subverting the original design and intention of standard music technologies, the artists and their audiences critique and resist aspects of the broader culture while creating space for joyous self-expression as they insist on living life at their own speed.

Looping time

Whereas cylinders, discs, and cassettes placed limits on musical duration, the tape loop offers nearly the opposite affordance—virtually unlimited playing time. The earliest loops were short lengths of quarter-inch-wide magnetic tape connected end to end, which, when played on a reel-to-reel machine, repeated whatever sounds were recorded on it over and over. In the twenty-first century, loops are more likely to be digital, activated by clicking a mouse, tapping a trackpad, pressing a synthesizer key, or hitting the rubberized pads of a drum machine or MIDI controller. The loop is a simple concept with unlimited musical possibilities. A loop can be accelerated or slowed, played backward or forward, layered on top of itself and combined with other loops; any short series of sounds—whether musical in origin or not—can become the basis of a new composition. But just as looping opens up new possibilities, it also reveals the constraints and unintended consequences that arise from the act of manipulating musical time.

The pioneering British electronic music composer Daphne Oram, who called the tape recorder "a remarkable piece of technology" and a "versatile instrument," created an ingenious form of sound synthesis in the early 1960s with loops of transparent 35mm filmstrips. She drew wavelike images in black ink on the film, which, when run through a large, purpose-built machine, synchronized the strips and converted the images into sound. She thus created music out of a recording medium in which no real-world sounds were actually recorded. A few years later, fellow Britons the Beatles (and their producers and engineers) used multiple manipulated tape loops to develop their psychedelic pop in songs such as "Tomorrow Never Knows" (1966), "Strawberry Fields Forever" (1967), and "Revolution 9" (1968). The high-pitched squawking in the beginning of "Tomorrow Never Knows," often described as the sound of a seagull, is a sped-up tape loop of Paul McCartney laughing.

Across the Atlantic and at about the same time, the US composer Steve Reich helped create the musical style known as minimalism through his experiments with tape loops, as in his pieces *It's Gonna Rain* (1965) and *Come Out* (1966). In these early pieces Reich played identical tape loops—often recordings of people speaking—on two reel-to-reel machines. Very gradually, the loops went out of synch, creating wholly unexpected musical effects that unfolded over several minutes. The composer memorably described what he heard in terms of physical movement: "ever so gradually, the sound moved over my left ear and then down my left side and then slithered across the floor and began to reverberate and really echo." The sense of linear movement, from point A to point B, is an illusion, ironically created by the circular motion of the loops, from point A to point A and back again.

In the 1970s another new form of music developed out of looping experiments: hip hop. Early hip hop loops came from DJs who manipulated short fragments of sound typically using two turntables. The fragments were usually short drum solos on funk and soul records called breaks. (The break from "Amen Brother," so central to drum and bass, had previously been showcased by hip hop DJs.) The DJs manually looped these breaks in a complex choreography of darting hands and rotating records. Playing the drum solo first on one turntable, they would then switch to the other machine just as the first break ended, quickly spin the first record backward to the beginning of the break, then return to it just as the other one ended, repeating these steps as desired or demanded. (This form of looping helped spur a new form of dance, known as breakdancing, breaking, or b-boying and b-girling.) Starting in the late 1980s the process of looping breaks could be automated—first through synthesizers and drum machines, then digital audiotape (DAT), and then software programs. In the digital age, the process of extracting sounds from existing recordings came to be known as sampling; much of what is often considered the golden age of hip hop in the late 1980s and early 1990s would not exist without looping and sampling. As Chuck D, the rapper and leader of the group Public Enemy, has said, "We put loops on top of loops on top of loops."

Yet another form of looping comes through the use of pedals, foot-operated devices attached to instruments or directly to a microphone. Digital looping pedals, or loopers, emerged in the 1980s, but it was not until the new millennium that they became more robust, versatile, inexpensive, and popular. Essentially live digital samplers, they can record, repeat, layer, and modify short phrases performed by a musician in real time. Scottish singer-songwriter KT Tunstall's 2010 live performance of her hit "Black Horse & the Cherry Tree" offers an example. After activating her looper with a tap of the foot, she thumps her guitar eight times, laying down a beat that will last through the rest of the performance. She pauses for two measures while the beat continues, then strums a short phrase on her guitar before adding four tambourine hits, all the while using her foot to operate an array of switches and pedals on the floor. She continues to build the layered introduction with handclaps and a "woo-hoo," repeated at two different pitch levels to allow her to sing in harmony with herself. Having constructed the rhythmic and harmonic framework, she moves into the verses and chorus, singing and strumming to the accompaniment of her digitally created one-woman backing band.

When Tunstall performed this song in 2010, her use of the looping pedal was commonplace, but its possibilities and impact were no less considerable because of it. Defying the laws of nature, the looping pedal allows performers to interact with their past selves; confounding our modern divisions of musical labor, it blurs the line between performing and composing. But at the same time that it opens up vast musical possibilities, the technology can also constrain: it encourages regular phrasing, a steady tempo, and a type of musical form in which a piece takes shape by adding and subtracting layers. Of course, it is possible to push back against these constraints. Indeed, we celebrate users of technology— Daphne Oram, the Beatles, Steve Reich, or Public Enemy—who resist or simply disregard the intended affordances of a device or tool. Yet, more often than not, users follow the grain rather than cut against it. To say this is not to accept technological determinism but to recognize that we work with tools and within systems whose design, options, and limitations are not of our own making, all of which shape our relationship with technology.

Our relationship with technology is also and always influenced by our socioeconomic realities, a fact that the looping pedal clearly illustrates. Where musicians have no financial support from government, industry, or private patronage, tools like the looping pedal have been embraced for their liberatory possibilities. The looper enables a kind of solo music making that would have once required multiple collaborators of different types, whether bandmates or recording engineers.

Practically speaking, a looping pedal can mean that an artist need not seek out, coordinate schedules with, or divide performance revenues among musical collaborators. For those who have been excluded from established networks or marginalized by mainstream society in general, any technology that allows self-sufficiency can mean the difference between having a career in music and having none. Women who have developed their craft through looping pedals have cited sexism—and their desire to avoid discrimination—as an important factor in their adoption of the technology. Returning to the 2010 performance of KT Tunstall, it is hard not to notice the two men sitting idly onstage, one staring at the floor, hands steepled, the other cradling a mute guitar. Although they seem to be sidelined bandmates, they happen to be two well-known soloists, David Gray and Ray LaMontagne, waiting their turn to perform. Regardless, the symbolism of their silence is palpable as they listen to Tunstall's self-reliant performance and performance of self-reliance.

We may justifiably applaud the freedom made possible by the looping pedal, but we should be mindful of unintended consequences. What is the impact of musically interacting with digital replications of oneself rather than with other musicians? Does the self-sufficiency that is made possible by loopers displace labor? How does the lowered barrier to entry for musicians affect supply and demand in the market? How might improvisation, whether solo or collective, change when using a device whose default function is exact repetition? In other words, when musicians build compositions and careers using looping pedals, who and what are left out of the loop? We should ask these types of questions about all influential forms of musical technologies. Doing so means that we should take neither a wholly celebratory nor a wholly critical stance toward technology and train ourselves to cast a skeptical eye on uncompromising praise or condemnation.

Countless technologies have shaped our engagement with musical time over the centuries. Debates have long raged about their use and impact, exposing a constant tension between competing values. But to reiterate a vital point, the value of music technology resides not solely in the objects themselves, however much one may want to curse a metronome for its intrusiveness or bless quantization for its help in the recording studio. Our curses and blessings tell us something more profound: that music technologies have served as an enduring means for wrestling with the realities of time, both ever-changing and eternal.

Chapter 4
Space

One morning, I walked down a busy London street while listening to downtempo music on my headphones. The business people heading toward me seemed to take on the character of the song, Radiohead's "Paranoid Android." I sensed despair as they trudged to their offices, resignation in their hunched postures and heavy tread. I then repeated my short walk, this time replacing Radiohead with the bouncy, joyful finale from Dvořák's String Quartet no. 12. The suited Londoners now seemed to have a lightness in their stride, serene smiles on their lips. It was not just the people that seemed to change with the music. The world around them, the buildings and traffic and streets, took on a different cast when I switched my soundtrack. If you are able, try this experiment using contrasting music and the location of your choice. Observe your surroundings—how does the music affect what you see and how you feel?

I offer this experiment to make a simple point with significant ramifications: the technologies of music configure and reconfigure our relationship with space. In an age of electronic mediation, music is often decoupled from the physical context in which it was created. We can hear chanting that was recorded in a monastery as we hurtle through the skies in an airplane; listen to chamber music while strolling in the woods; enjoy a Bollywood showstopper during a taxi ride. But music has been traveling far and wide for much longer than portable players have existed. Earlier technologies, particularly notation and printing, made it possible for music to move across distances and cultures, and the circulation of music has allowed for the circulation of aesthetics, values, and power. But even when music stays rooted in place, it influences our sense of the spaces in which we encounter it. At the same time these spaces, whether caves, cathedrals, or concert halls, shape how we create and hear music.

Caves, cathedrals, and concert halls: architectural acoustics

In the early twenty-first century, site-specific music—created in response to and intended to be performed in a particular physical space—is the exception, often the province of avant-garde composers or sound artists. This was not always the case. Music making was typically tied to indoor or outdoor spaces, whether temples or taverns, forests or the open sea, mountaintops or symphony halls. The size, shape, and construction of these spaces all affected how people experienced music within them. Millennia before the science of acoustics was developed, humans were manipulating spaces to meet their musical needs and creating music that suited the acoustic qualities of those spaces. The manipulation and engagement with architectural acoustics, as it is now called, mediates both sound and meaning.

Researchers studying caves in southern France and northern Spain discovered tantalizing connections between the placement of Paleolithic art and the resonant qualities of the caves themselves. Cave art was often placed in locations where speech, song, or instrumental performance would be amplified most powerfully or pleasingly, and it is speculated that important rituals would have taken place in front of the art for maximum effect. The connection between natural acoustics and art was essential for these cave dwellers, a term that belies their sophisticated interaction with their environment. There is good evidence that prehistoric humans treated caves as tools to amplify their expressive and spiritual impulses. Likely they discovered the musicality of caves accidentally. Water dripping onto a stone floor or a knuckle rapping a rock formation can produce ringing tones, and these sounds may have sparked the imaginations of our ancestors. Rocks that resonate when struck—known as lithophones—were some of our earliest instruments; caves were among our first indoor music venues.

The early history of European classical music can be understood in part as developing in response to the architectural features and changing acoustics of performance spaces, particularly churches. The Notre Dame Cathedral in Paris, built over the course of more than a century starting in 1163, is where polyphony (the simultaneous sounding of multiple independent musical lines) began to flourish in the Western tradition. Music was frequently sung in Notre Dame as it was being constructed, and when, for example, the addition of the transept and nave greatly expanded the space, composers and performers had to adjust to the new acoustics but could also exploit new musical possibilities. Although we can only speculate at this point, it is likely that important developments in Western polyphony arose in response to the changing size and shape of this landmark church.

St. Mark's Basilica (Basilica di San Marco), Venice's most famous church, played a significant role in the music of the Italian Renaissance. The two widely spaced marble lofts added in the 1540s enabled pieces to be written for multiple choirs or instrumental ensembles and inspired techniques that created a stereo-like effect. Renowned composers including Adrian Willaert, Andrea and Giovanni Gabrieli, and Claudio Monteverdi wrote some of the most revered works of the Renaissance era specifically to be performed within the distinctive architecture of St. Mark's.

The baroque churches of seventeenth- and eighteenth-century Germany equally inspired and influenced the composers in their hire. The heavily ornamented and often curved surfaces diffused sound and generally shortened reverberation times as compared to Gothic and Renaissance structures. The "drier" acoustics of these spaces permitted composers to write more complex polyphony and allowed performers to add a profusion of musical ornamentation to their playing without muddying the sound. J. S. Bach, an employee of the St. Thomas Church (Thomaskirche) in Leipzig, Germany, from 1723 to 1750, composed hundreds of works to be performed in this space, no doubt responding to the sonic qualities of the architecture as he wrote to order for its organ and for the ensembles that regularly performed there.

It was not until the eighteenth century that the first purpose-built musical venues started to appear in Europe, and they multiplied considerably in the 1800s and 1900s. For centuries, music performed in large indoor spaces—houses of worship, palaces, and the like—tended to be in the service of veneration, whether toward ancestors, deities, or rulers. These new concert halls may be thought of as secular temples that venerated composers and their creations. The nineteenth century saw the reconception of the composer as a revered, almost godlike figure, their names and busts adorning the walls of these halls.

All musical spaces, from caves to cathedrals to concert halls, influence the creation and experience of music within them. They direct the attention of listeners, shape the actions of artists and audiences, and convey a sense of intimacy or of vastness. Buildings and other structures are forms of technology that can be refined and adjusted, built for specific musical purposes or adapted to evolving needs and tastes. Ironically, they loom large in a physical sense but tend to be underappreciated forces in the development of music; they are, however, musical technologies as vital as any other.

Notation: tonic sol-fa as a tool for education and empire

Notation is a form of music technology, a tool that enables the preservation and transmission of knowledge and ideas through a system of symbols. It has existed for millennia, an early example coming from a 3,400-year-old tablet found in what is now Iraq. Notation exists in endless variety, employing abstract symbols, written language, and representational figures; written by hand, printed, or generated through code; preserved in clay, parchment, paper, and computer graphics. Player piano rolls, perforated with holes that activate the instrument's keys, are a form of notation, as are the color-coded blocks representing different sounds on DAWs (digital audio workstations). Notation captures sound in its lines and shapes and colors, allowing music to exist outside the act of performance, giving it a freedom of movement. Notation allowed the printing of music to exist, and with replicable symbols music could be mass-produced and circulated in ways that expensive, handwritten manuscripts could not.

The only form of music preservation in the centuries before the phonograph, notation has affected every aspect of how music is created, disseminated, and experienced. As with any form of information technology, notation has been used to promote empowerment and education and the unfettered spread of knowledge, and it has been used to subjugate and to colonize. We can see both in operation in the way that a nineteenth-century English system of notation, tonic sol-fa, came to be used around the world.

Sarah Anna Glover was a Sunday school teacher in Norwich, England, in the early nineteenth century. She ardently believed that singing was a public good and that everyone should be able to sing not just by ear but also by reading notation. Glover sought a method that did not require young students to decipher all the symbols of Western music notation. Drawing on practices dating to the tenth century, she created a simplified form of notation that did away with staves, clefs, note heads, and the like and replaced them with letters that stood in for the traditional syllables used to represent pitches. Do, re, me, fa, sol, la, and ti became d, r, m, and so on; rhythm was indicated via a combination of spacing and punctuation marks.

Tonic sol-fa was adopted widely throughout England and soon came to be aligned with movements to end societal ills. The temperance movement employed music to reinforce its antialcohol message, and tonic sol-fa became a critical tool for teaching and disseminating their songs. English missionaries saw the value of the notation, which was simpler to teach and learn in places around the world where English was not widely spoken. The London Missionary Society adopted tonic sol-fa starting in 1862, soon after sending a missionary to Madagascar to teach Christian hymns with it.

The use of tonic sol-fa among missionaries around the world coincided with—and aided—British imperialism over the course of many decades, stretching well into the twentieth century. Reports from Nigeria, South Africa, Zimbabwe, China, and Fiji noted with great excitement how music could "tame" and "subdue," "conquer," and "discipline" the local people, who were frequently described as "savages." Tonic sol-fa was a principal means of teaching music and the values embedded in the lyrics of the songs that accompanied them. Music was considered part of a civilizing project that served the best interests of the colonized, but often the opposite was the case. Historian Mhoze Chikowero writes of the impact of tonic sol-fa in Zimbabwe: "The overreliance on sol-fa meant the music remained foreign and that Africans were actively schooled into musical illiteracy."

The power of tonic sol-fa was its simplicity, which aided its spread, first within England and then around the world. All forms of notation simplify and reduce, representing certain aspects of sound while excluding or minimizing others. When one form of notation encounters a musical tradition that it was not designed to represent, we can see the limitations of notation and the potential for misrepresentation. This is laid bare in the long tradition of Western scholars attempting to transcribe examples from musical traditions outside the twelve-note tonal system. In Arabic music, for example, there are notes found between the half steps of the twelve-note scale that cannot easily be represented by Western staff notation, especially given that the intervals between notes do not always accord to the even fractions implied by sharp and flat signs. Western notation can foster an appreciation of music and the cultures and people they represent. But when it fails to capture the richness and complexity of a musical tradition, a transcription can be taken as false evidence of primitiveness or unsophistication. As notation moves through space and across borders, it becomes a case study of how technology facilitates encounters between cultures and traditions and how these encounters expose and reinforce values and power relationships.

Music in public and private spaces: the boom box and the Walkman

The twentieth century introduced many ways to explore the relationship between music and space. Consider two, the boom box and the Walkman, both of which became popular in the 1980s. Neither represented a technological breakthrough. The boom box brought together two existing technologies, the transistor radio (introduced in the 1950s) and the cassette player (from the 1960s), adding large speakers. The Walkman was just a cassette player with lightweight headphones; radio was added later. Both ran on standard batteries and were designed to be portable, the boom box by virtue of its handle, the Walkman because of its small size. What made these technologies distinctive was how they increased the power, flexibility, and quality of portable music. Although beloved by generations of users, the transistor radio—the main form of personal, portable music before the 1980s—had a relatively small sound, often described as "tinny," and it could not play cassette tapes, limiting the range of musical options. By contrast, the boom box could play music at a much higher volume and the Walkman improved on its predecessor's sound quality; and both bestowed upon listeners the ability to listen to music of their choice, when and where they chose. Moreover, the boom box and the Walkman—because of their affordances and their widespread popularity—challenged the boundaries between public and private space and the role that music played within these spaces.

The boom box was essentially a home stereo system made moveable. As a 1980 advertisement pointed out, "this Panasonic stereo has one component your component system doesn't have. A handle." Although boom boxes could be taken just about anywhere, in the United States they became notable for their use in crowded cityscapes and have a special connection with Black and Latinx youth during the early years of hip hop. They were symbols of empowerment and transgression, allowing disenfranchised young people to claim public spaces as their own—without permission or great expense. Boom boxes blasted in parks and playgrounds, on buses and subway cars, and in the hands of their owners as they walked down busy streets. Because of this, they were also seen as disturbers of the peace, imposing unwanted music on others. In Spike Lee's 1989 film *Do the Right Thing*, a boom box serves as a symbol of not only power and resistance, but also provocation and division. In key scenes, a Promax "Super Jumbo" boom box figures in a sonic battle between a Black teenager named Radio Raheem and a group of Puerto Rican youth, as well as in a violent encounter between Raheem and a white restaurant owner. The song that constantly plays on the boom box is laden with symbolism: Public Enemy's "Fight the Power." (Radio Raheem was inspired by a person known as "Joe Radio" who roamed the streets of Spike Lee's Brooklyn neighborhood with a transistor radio on his shoulder.)

6. A Promax Super Jumbo boom box used in the 1989 film *Do the Right Thing*. The boom box figures prominently throughout, most notably when the character Radio Raheem brings it into Sal's Pizzeria and a violent confrontation with the restaurant's owner ensues.

Like the boom box, the portable personal cassette player—often referred to generically by its brand name, Walkman—provoked strong sentiment about the role of music in public spaces. Introduced by the Japanese company Sony in 1979, the original device came with two headphone jacks, encouraging users to share their music. The Walkman, however, came to represent the ultimate in musical individualism, allowing its owners to move through the world accompanied by soundtracks created for and heard by an audience of one. Fans loved the convenience, the freedom, and the ability to be in the world but be sonically separated from it. Critics found the device unsettling, narcissistic, a renunciation of community and societal norms. Local laws were even enacted across the United States in the early 1980s that levied fines against those who wore headphones while driving, bicycling, or even crossing the street as a pedestrian. These laws were meant to promote safety, but they also represented a critique of the technology. The Walkman enjoyed its heyday in the 1980s, but its descendants, including portable CD and MP3 players such as the Discman and iPod, multiplied to the extent that portable music players, and thus public earphone wearing, became more popular than ever in the first decades of the twenty-first century. As mobile phones started to serve as primary music players, private listening in public became even more prevalent. But with short-range wireless technology (particularly in the form of the Bluetooth standard) and with earbuds shrinking in size, it becomes more difficult to discern who among us is listening to their own private soundtrack. We are still figuring out the social norms around private–public listening, and the disappearance of obvious visible markers (large boom boxes, headphones, and wires) only complicates matters. As portable music technologies proliferate and evolve, we find ourselves continually reconfiguring our relationship with public and private space and reconsidering the distinctions between them.

As always, culture plays a decisive factor in the use and value of music technologies, and this was true in the case of the boom box and the Walkman. In the United States, boom boxes are less visible (and audible) in the twenty-first century, no longer provoking the kind of embrace or backlash they once did. In the late 1980s, boom boxes were frequently called "ghetto blasters" in the United States. The term, which could be celebratory or derogatory, highlighted the intersection of race and space that this technology occupied. But move from twentieth-century New York to twenty-first-century Bangalore, India, or Hangzhou, China, and the issues change. In Bangalore, a large, crowded city like New York and Hangzhou, boom boxes are common but tend to stay rooted to public places, most often shops or market stalls, while headphone wearing is more of a novelty. MP3 players and mobile phones often serve the same purpose as boom boxes, connected to small speakers rather than earbuds for personal use. The music booming from these boxes, both small and large, is often drawn from the genre of Bollywood film music, evoking the imagery and dance routines so frequently connected to the films. To encounter this mix of open-air music combined with the sounds of busy city life is to experience what musicologist Sindhumathi Revuluri calls "outloud listening," a collective and public experience of sound distinct from the more individualized listening common in many Western urban cultures.

In the late 1990s, Hangzhou became known for its "dancing grannies." Although seemingly innocuous and charming to many, the gathering of older women in Hangzhou's parks and other public spaces to dance and exercise to music played on portable stereos created intergenerational conflict. Residents called the authorities to report these gatherings as public disturbances. Young men wanting to play basketball or hang out complained about being displaced. Sonic battles erupted as annoyed citizens tried to drown out the grannies with their own boom boxes. In the years since the phenomenon became popular in Hangzhou, it has spread throughout China; a 2015 report estimated the dancing grannies at 100 million strong. In large Chinese cities, the boom box has come to symbolize a confluence of cultural and economic factors, among them the decreasing cost and ready availability of Chinese-manufactured electronics, intergenerational conflict, and a clash between traditional collectivism and modern individualism.

Fugitive music: X-ray records and El Paquete Semanal

Trenchcoated black marketeers sold them in back alleys in cities across Russia. They could cost a day's or even a week's salary, or the equivalent in vodka. The government flooded the market with fakes to depress sales, but demand continued. Dealers were arrested, sometimes imprisoned. Made and circulated between the mid 1940s and mid 1960s, these items were an ingenious and macabre form of bootlegged records. Often referred to as bones (костяк) or ribs (ребра), they were recordings made out of used X-ray film. With bony fingers splayed across the surface of the disc or ghostly skulls staring eyeless, the discs trapped nightmarish creatures within their grooves. The music, however, was full of life, often jazz and rock and roll from the West, all the more thrilling for being so scarce in the Soviet Union.

After World War II, when most of the raw material for making records in the USSR was reserved for the state record label, Melodiya, someone, somehow discovered that used X-rays could be a serviceable substitute. (The material resembled that of flexi discs, thin plastic recordings that often accompanied magazines or books, which had their heyday in the 1960s and 1970s.) Bootleggers retrieved them from trash bins behind hospitals or obtained them by bribing technicians. The discs were usually seven inches in diameter, the size of a 45 rpm record, but they were recorded at 78 rpm, usually holding a single song. Rather than being pressed, as with traditional discs, X-ray records were inscribed with cutting tools, or lathes, often copying commercially made discs that were smuggled into the country. Underground record labels emerged, the most famous being the Golden Dog Gang. (The name was a reference to Nipper, the dog depicted in the iconic logo of the British label HMV, His Master's Voice, which showed the canine staring into the horn of a gramophone as he listened to his owner speaking from it.) X-ray records could not be mass produced, and they often sounded terrible, degrading with every play. Nevertheless, these records circulated by the thousands for nearly twenty years. (Demand largely vanished after 1964 when Soviet citizens could obtain reel-to-reel tape machines and, with them, easier means to copy music.) During those years, dedicated music fans persevered, tolerating the risk, expense, and noise that accompanied these bony discs. Manufacturing the records required considerable labor and ingenuity. A phenomenon fueled by scarcity, secrecy, and passion, X-ray records reveal one of the fascinating ways in which music travels through the world, sometimes through contested territory and at great risk, driven by technology and desire.

Several decades later, another ingenious form of musical dissemination arose in what had been one of the USSR's staunchest allies. Cuba's El Paquete Semanal, or the weekly package, is a form of what is called a sneakernet. It is an offline form of the Internet, a tongue-in-cheek term to describe the circulation of digital content by physical, in-person distribution, often transported by foot—thus sneakernet. El Paquete supplements, even replaces, the traditional online form of the Internet for millions of people in Cuba, where few have reliable, fast Internet access. Every week, and operating since about 2011, new content travels across the island's twelve provinces, from the busy streets of the capital, Havana, to the remotest countryside, on portable drives, CDs, and DVDs. El Paquete is not a government-sanctioned enterprise, but its strict lack of antigovernment material and pornography suggests that it is condoned, perhaps even facilitated to an extent, by the state. El Paquete Semanal is much cheaper than online access in Cuba, and consumers can economize by purchasing portions of the package, sharing content, and reusing USB drives. Still, for many, El Paquete can cost the equivalent of one or more days' salary. Content includes television shows, films, instructional videos, apps, classified advertising, and, of course, music.

El Paquete Semanal is a network of curators and compilers, distributors and consumers with three main nodes: *los maestros* (the masters), *los paqueteros* (the packagers), and *la gente* (the people). *Los maestros* acquire, compile, and organize the content, often working in studios of subject-matter experts, each responsible for a different part of the package. *Los paqueteros* are the distributors. Some of them set up storefronts, but many have jobs that require local or national travel—taxi drivers and mobile food vendors, for example—who sell the weekly packages on their routes. *La gente* are the consumers, the millions of Cubans who buy the package.

Those responsible for the music section of El Paquete are powerful figures, serving as gatekeepers and promoters. Some of them have become famous, even to the extent that their photos—not the performers'—may be featured on an album's cover art. Although it might seem a top-down operation, *los paqueteros* and *la gente* play significant roles as musical curators and tastemakers. The packagers often know their clientele well and cater to particular individuals or groups (and add content of their own choosing) based on their musical tastes or needs, whether restaurant owners or religious music lovers. Nor are *la gente* passive recipients of El Paquete—they share and recommend music to each other, shaping consumption and taste as well.

In the second half of the 2010s, El Paquete constituted the largest information network in Cuba and was the country's biggest employer, representing a significant alternative form of digital music distribution. It operated largely outside monopolistic or oligopolistic corporate control; the algorithms that powerfully (and often invisibly) shape the consumption of listeners in wealthier countries exercised much less power over Cuban consumers. Although power is not distributed equally across El Paquete, it is shared among members of the community, often at a very local level. Still, El Paquete is not a model of utopian music sharing because it was a response to isolation, deprivation, and repression. Like the X-ray music of the Cold War Soviet Union, El Paquete Semanal reveals the irrepressible human need to share music, to find ever new routes for it to travel, whatever the challenges, whatever the risk.

Music is often thought of primarily as an art form that exists in time, but its relationship with space is equally vital. Even in perhaps its simplest setting—a person singing alone—music travels through space, and once that happens technology comes into play. From the early humans who used the structure of caves to magnify their voices and express their beliefs to our more recent ancestors who created or manipulated larger, more ornate settings to suit their expressive needs, our music has been shaped by the spaces in which it resounds.

Powerful singers can project their voices across hundreds of feet; traveling musicians can spread their music across hundreds or thousands of miles. Humans have long sought to expand musical mobility, to extend the range of music beyond what performers can achieve in live, acoustic performance. Countless sheep and trees have given their lives over the centuries so that humans could record symbols on parchment and paper and spread their music to faraway lands or to bring distant music home. Music boxes, first developed in eighteenth-century Switzerland, traveled the world more than a century before phonograph recordings and radio spun and beamed music inside homes and across oceans. In Poland during the Cold War, sound postcards, *pocztówki dźwiękowe*, contained flexible discs that, like Soviet X-ray records, allowed scarce popular music to circulate among eager listeners. In 1973, Bhutan developed a novel way of sending music through the mail—by issuing tiny records as stamps. The Himalayan kingdom outdid itself in 2008 and 2009 with a set of CD stamps. And then there is NASA's Golden Records, twelve-inch gold-plated copper records that are traveling through the cosmos. Two copies of the disc were created by the US space agency in 1977, containing recordings of music representing a variety of Earth's cultures, one each placed in the two *Voyager* spacecrafts. Human-made music has now left the solar system, billions of miles from the home planet.

Music had already been traveling intangibly across the world with radio, but with the widespread emergence of the Internet in the 1990s, a new era of musical mobility dawned. File-sharing and downloading and then streaming have allowed many millions to pluck music from anywhere in the world and listen to it on their computers and mobile devices. But as with the example of El Paquete Semanal, digital music can move freely even where there is little Internet connectivity. In many places, such as the desert regions of Mali, music is widely traded via mobile phone SIM cards.

These ever-developing technologies shape the way we hear music and how we interpret its meaning and function. They affect access, spreading the influence of musical traditions and practices, serving education and entertainment, colonization, and propaganda. As new technologies emerge, they challenge traditional boundaries and complicate the distinction between public and private. But just as these technologies complicate and expand our relationship with music, they continue to serve long-held human desires—to have music ever at hand and to spread it far and wide.

Chapter 5
Community

Listening to music alone was once a rarity. Yes, one could always sing or play for oneself, and starting in the eighteenth century, mechanical music boxes made it possible to listen to music alone without making it. But otherwise, anytime people heard music it was in the presence of other people. Music was, almost inescapably, a communal experience, that is, until the early twentieth century, when phonographs and radios became household items. In the twenty-first century, with ever cheaper and smaller headphones and portable players, perhaps billions of people regularly listen to music by themselves. Given the ubiquity of solitary listening, we might think that technology has had an inevitably isolating effect on the way we experience music. And yet, it has also been harnessed as a means to convene people around music. In a testament to the deeply rooted human need for community, an array of music technologies has been developed and deployed since the turn of the twentieth century to serve our desire to create and experience music together.

Telephone concerts, phonograph parties, and radio exercise

On March 12, 1878, an unusual concert was held in Corinthian Hall in Rochester, New York. The program that night, held on the same stage that had hosted luminaries such as Frederick Douglass and Ralph Waldo Emerson, featured three performers playing just six short pieces—four songs and two cornet solos. The music was standard fare and the performers were hardly famous. What distinguished the program was the mode by which the music was delivered. The musicians were nowhere in sight. In fact, they were seventy miles west in Buffalo, New York, playing in front of a telephone. Billed as a "Grand Telephone Concert," the event was meant to illustrate the wonders of the 1876 invention by demonstrating the near-miraculous feat of gathering an audience in one city to hear a concert performed in another. Similar events were held around the country and later in Europe. (In France, the *théâtrophone* was a service that connected distant listeners to opera and theater performances over telephone wires, operating from 1890 to 1932.) Audiences cheered and critics praised the technology, but what most impressed spectators was that it could happen at all. Technical difficulties plagued the proceedings, and the quality of the sound was often poor. A *New York Times* review captured the mixed response: "As a novelty, [it] was highly entertaining, though, unless an almost incredible improvement be effected, it is difficult to see how the transmission of music over the new instrument can be of permanent or practical value."

On the evening of the Rochester "Grand Telephone Concert," another new technology shared the stage: the phonograph. The final part of the program was announced as follows: "Recitations, Conversational Remarks, Animal Mimicry, Laughing, Coughing, etc., etc., will be re-produced by the Phonograph with such fidelity of tone, articulation, emphasis, etc. as to satisfy the most skeptical that this apparatus is really a great discovery, and not a mere trick or toy producing deceptive effects." What was not included in this "Exhibition of the Phonograph" was music. The technology was less than a year old, and its uses were still being explored and negotiated. At this point, the demonstration was apparently designed to prove a negative—that the phonograph was not "a mere trick or toy."

Over the ensuing decades, a consensus formed around a primary if not singular use of the phonograph as an instrument for the preservation, reproduction, and dissemination of music. As the cultural significance of the phonograph became more or less settled, it came to be incorporated into everyday musical life, and this is when we start to see gatherings around the phonograph that were no longer designed primarily as exhibitions or demonstrations, but meant to emulate traditional communal activities.

Consider, for example, an 1898 concert hosted in Lancaster, Pennsylvania. Commerce and entertainment seemed to be the dual purposes of the event. The evening featured the Columbia Graphophone, prominently advertised on the back page of the program. Surrounded by ads for cigars, paint, jewelry, and shoes was a list of thirty recordings in two parts. The pieces, played on cylinders, a medium that preceded (and coexisted with) flat discs, could only be about two minutes long. The program was a potpourri of styles—marches, polkas, and waltzes; vocal selections; pieces for banjo, piccolo, and xylophone; one speech; and two comic skits. Phonograph companies regularly featured these kinds of events in the early years of the industry, when familiar concert settings must have been seen as the best way to convince people to investigate—and buy—this technology.

Phonograph gatherings were not mounted merely to move merchandise. Over the early decades of the twentieth century, countless reports can be found of events designed as social or educational activities. In 1905, Felix Machray published a short article in a British journal describing a party at which he entertained an audience of nearly 200, playing a carefully curated set of pieces drawn from sixty records. The author relied on his musical knowledge and discernment but also tried to anticipate and respond to the audience's desires and tastes. Describing himself as a "phonoist," he was an early practitioner of an art designed to convene and create community through the curation of recorded sound, an art that had yet to receive its now common name, that of the disc jockey, or DJ.

Machray may not have been playing dance music, but many proto-DJs did, and phonograph enthusiasts delighted at how easily and cheaply they could gather people to shake and shimmy. As a 1924 article in a US housekeeping magazine touted, "an informal dancing party can be given with no preparation more difficult than rolling up the rugs and calling in the neighbors, while the best orchestras in the world, Paul Whiteman's, Art Hickman's, Confrey's and McKee's, are on call." The industry encouraged the trend with endless advertisements, many with images of exuberant dancers. "The best friend of a hostess is a Victrola," one oft-seen ad announced, referring to one of the most popular brands of phonograph. Several commentators directly linked the increased popularity of social dancing to recorded sound. As a British journal observed in 1923, "few people will deny that the dance craze, which now holds everyone literally in its grip, owes nearly everything to the gramophone."

In addition to phonograph parties—which sometimes also included making recordings as well as listening to them—we find social gatherings designed to edify or educate. As so often is the case, the new technology was incorporated into preexisting cultural practices. In middle-class US society this meant bringing the phonograph into same-gender gatherings and organizations such as women's and men's clubs. When Alice B. Talbot moved north from Philadelphia to a small town in Maine in the 1920s, she discovered that classical music was not well known in the community. So she convened a "girls' class in music appreciation," and over the course of dozens of Saturday afternoons she introduced young women to European classical music—often referred to as "good music"—with her phonograph and record collection.

Music and Technology

BOOM .. boom ..
the beat of the
bass

CLEAR and strong, the voice of the Orthophonic Victrola beats out the deep measures that inspire good dancing. Such tone, such volume, such compelling rhythm were never heard before. Now you can roll up the rugs and bring the thrill of a ballroom orchestra to your living-room. Neither the shuffling feet of ten, or twenty, or thirty couples— nor their merry repartee—can rise above the booming beat of Orthophonic bass.

The Orthophonic Victrola stands alone in reproducing the throbbing, beating rhythm that characterizes the dance music of the day. It drives the booming of the double basses, the steady notes of the drums, the dynamic tubas through the din of the gayest party and makes magic out of all dance music, no matter what is played.

Today—see and hear the beautiful new models of the Orthophonic Victrola—the Credenza at $300—the Granada at $150— the Colony at $110, and the Consolette at $85. Any dealer in Victor products will gladly give you a demonstration—*today*.

Send for free pamphlet
describing the miracle of the new Orthophonic Victrola. Just send your name and address to the Victor Talking Machine Company, Camden, New Jersey, and a pamphlet describing the interesting development of the Orthophonic Victrola will be sent to you free of charge.

*The New
Orthophonic* Victrola

VICTOR TALKING MACHINE COMPANY   CAMDEN, NEW JERSEY, U. S. A.

7. A 1926 advertisement for the Victrola Orthophonic phonograph emphasized the machine's suitability for social dancing. The image shows two people rolling up a rug to make space for the impromptu gathering, while dancers of different generations are already in motion.

Gramophone societies first emerged in England in the 1910s, becoming phonograph societies as the phenomenon crossed the Atlantic in the 1920s. These organizations allowed men to socialize around music and technology. Their activities included demonstrations of the latest equipment and discussions of music and records. A 1926 report from the Minneapolis Phonograph Society explained how community formed around shared interests: "These ardent gramophiles discovered each other; found, with mingled surprise and delight, that their passion was by no means isolated and that there were others in the city similarly touched. Music, we feel, and the discussion of music, is the raison d'être of our organization." These societies flourished over the next several years, eventually (and often reluctantly) admitting women. In England, they continued to meet well into the twenty-first century, upholding a legacy of nearly a century and a half of socializing around the phonograph.

Radio exercise in Japan

In 1923, an official from Japan's Ministry of Communication traveled to the United States on a fact-finding mission. One initiative especially impressed him—Metropolitan Life Insurance Company, he learned, was developing a radio program meant to promote exercise. Another ministry official followed up on the original visit in 1927 and reported on its fifteen-minute broadcasts in which announcers, accompanied by piano music, called out exercises to their listeners. Convinced of the value of the idea, the ministry developed its own program and in 1928, *rajio taisō*— radio exercise—was born.

Radio exercise was modestly successful in the United States, and its successors—exercise records, cassette tapes, videocassettes, CDs, DVDs, and online videos—did brisk business over the following decades. But in Japan, the concept became part of its national ethos and identity. NHK, Japan's national broadcasting corporation, aired ten-minute programs multiple times daily. The postal service

8. A 1928 Japanese pamphlet provided instructions for *rajio taisō*, or radio exercise. The text, in part, reads, "A family's health, a family's happiness. The whole family gathers to do *Rajio taisō*."

circulated millions of illustrated pamphlets to encourage citizens to learn the exercises. Schoolchildren and factory workers across the country stopped their studies and work and started doing calisthenics at the appointed times. Loudspeakers were set up in public parks and in the center of small towns, ensuring that everyone, wherever they might be, could hear the program.

Although the exercises—gentle movements accessible to almost anyone—can be accompanied by different types of music, there is a distinctive *rajio taisō* sound. It is the sound of a piano, played at a moderate pace with plodding quarter notes in the left hand and lilting eighth notes in the right. Remaining resolutely in major keys, the music offers no rhythmic or harmonic complexities. The first *rajio taisō* piece was written by composer and educator Naoki Fukui, who in 1929 founded Musashino Academia Musicae, a conservatory in Tokyo. The piece now most closely associated with *rajio taisō* was penned in 1951 by Tadashi Hattori, a prolific composer who also wrote scores for films by the famous Japanese director Akira Kurosawa.

Hattori's untitled piece is known by generations and millions of Japanese people. It may be the most familiar, most widely heard piece of Japanese music, even more ubiquitous than the country's national anthem. The music continues to be heard regularly well into the twenty-first century, appearing in television shows and video games and accompanying countless online videos, including ones posted during the coronavirus pandemic and led by mask-wearing instructors.

Although *rajio taisō* was designed to promote better health in Japan, it was from the beginning a form of technologically assisted community building. It was meant to strengthen ties to one's local school, factory, office, neighborhood, or park. Just as important, it was created to foster a sense of national community and identity, one that valued not just good health, but also efficiency, punctuality, and precision. The "Japaneseness" of *rajio taisō* manifested in other ways as well. Exercises were held in Buddhist and Shinto temples, and often the loudspeakers in parks were designed to emulate the *tōrō*, a stone lantern seen in temples, shrines, and traditional gardens. The connection between *rajio taisō* and Japanese identity was clearly perceived by the forces that occupied Japan after its defeat in World War II. The Allied powers must have seen *rajio taisō* as a threat, perhaps a way to unite the Japanese people against the occupiers, and instituted a ban that lasted until 1951. Those who led the occupation likely had no idea that the practice they banned had been inspired by a US innovation. By this time, however, radio exercise was a Japanese cultural phenomenon, an inextricable part of community life throughout the nation.

Karaoke

New technologies always emerge out of robust, preexisting cultural contexts that inevitably inform their use and meaning.

This was true of *rajio taisō*, and it was also the case with karaoke, which emerged in the early 1970s in Japan but then traveled the world. Combining elements of two venerable Japanese traditions, impromptu singing at social gatherings and singing contests, karaoke was created to facilitate social singing by providing professionally recorded accompaniment. The fundamental feature of any karaoke technology—whether employing cassettes, CDs, laser discs, music videos, MP3s, or some other format—is that the recordings it plays are not complete in themselves. The very term *karaoke*, roughly translated as "empty orchestra," points to this incompleteness. Simply insofar as karaoke *demands* active music participation, it provides a counterexample to the common argument that recording technology fosters a passive relationship with music. It also exemplifies how technologies can be created for or adapt to communal music activities. Although rooted in Japanese tradition, karaoke can easily be incorporated into different contexts since amateur singing in social settings is common practically everywhere. Indeed, it was not long before the practice was embraced around the world.

When karaoke left home, it tended to settle first in Japanese expatriate communities. This was the case in the United Kingdom, where karaoke machines initially appeared in restaurants and nightclubs that catered to Japanese clientele. It started to gain national attention in 1989 through a television program called Kazuko's Karaoke Club. The host, Japanese singer Kazuko Hohki, interviewed celebrities, plied them with alcohol, and then had them sing along to the backing of a cassette tape–playing karaoke machine. Karaoke was clearly unfamiliar to the audience, to whom she explained the meaning of the word and introduced the features of the machine.

Over the next few years, karaoke, no longer a curiosity, came to take a prominent place in British culture. Its increasing popularity owed a great deal to existing traditions rooted in amateur communal singing among the working class, particularly within pubs. The practice of what are called sing-songs or sing-alongs in pubs is centuries old, but their popularity surged in the early and mid-1800s. Some pubs designated rooms called free-and-easies or singing saloons, typically hosting both solo and group singing, with more participants joining in as the night wore on and the beer flowed.

When karaoke arrived in late-twentieth-century Britain, the glory days of pub singing had long passed. This Japanese import revitalized the nearly dormant practice. In the 1990s, British karaoke came into its own, typically featuring British and US pop hits as well as traditional folk tunes and iconic football (soccer) songs. Another existing tradition brought into British karaoke was the practice of ending a session with group singing, which is less common in Japan. A longtime favorite is "You'll Never Walk Alone," from the Rodgers and Hammerstein musical *Carousel*, an American song that became quintessentially British after the Liverpudlian band Gerry and the Pacemakers covered it in 1963. Its secure place in karaoke playlists across Britain—along with songs like Queen's "We Are the Champions" (1977) and the ballad "Danny Boy"—attests to the adaptability of music technologies as they travel around the world.

The history of karaoke in Brazil began much the same way it did in Britain, first gaining a foothold in Japanese bars, clubs, and restaurants and then becoming popular among the broader population. But because Brazil has the largest Japanese population outside Japan—vastly larger than Britain's—and because of the long and ongoing movement of Japanese people between the two countries, Brazil was an early adopter. Karaoke had gained national media attention by 1977, more than a decade before it was well known in Britain.

The existence of such a large Japanese Brazilian population shaped the development of karaoke in Brazil. For one, the *Nipo-brasileiros* or *japonês*, as they are called, tend to sing karaoke in Japanese—often sentimental *enka* ballads—even if they do not speak the language. Most notable is the extensive network of karaoke clubs, classes, and contests run by Japanese Brazilian organizations. São Paulo—the center of the Japanese immigrant population—has been home to well over 100 such clubs. They organize events and offer instruction, often by professional singers. Since the early 1990s, the União Paulista de Karaoke, or the Karaoke Union of São Paulo, has overseen a busy calendar of competitions. These events, inspired by the Japanese tradition of singing contests known as *nodojiman* (literally, "boasting throat"), feature monetary prizes, dozens of categories, hundreds of participants, and strict rules. The Japanese Brazilian karaoke network is said to rival or exceed Japan's in terms of robustness and complexity; it reflects a tendency among immigrant populations around the world to adhere to customs or traditions more strictly than is observed in the land of their ancestors.

In Brazil, the karaoke tradition of *Nipo-brasileiros* is well known and well respected. The reception of Japanese Brazilians tends to be quite different when they visit or relocate to Japan. In Japan, they are typically regarded as *gaijin*, or foreigners, and may face negative stereotypes and discrimination. For Japanese Brazilians in Japan, karaoke also serves to build community, but they often sing in Portuguese, drawing on Brazilian songs and genres; there, karaoke helps combat homesickness and can serve as a way to insulate themselves from a harsh environment. Whether in Japan, Britain, Brazil, or any of the scores of countries that have embraced karaoke, the technology of the empty orchestra facilitates the sharing of identities, histories, and values, and in so many varied and often unexpected ways.

Online musical community

A community is a social formation in which shared beliefs, identities, interests, practices, and values connect members and generate group activities, norms, and structures. Traditionally, communities are geographically bound, their activities and events unfolding synchronously, their members interacting in each other's physical presence. Community can also exist online. But given the distinctive nature of virtual space and interactions, how do online communities foster belonging, connection, and solidarity? The short answer is that community building happens, just as in the physical world, through communication and sharing. The difference is in how people communicate and share—mediated rather than immediate, digital rather than analog, asynchronously as well as synchronously.

Rather than primarily speaking (physically) face to face, online communities communicate through email, chat spaces, comment sections, and other text-based platforms; through voice-only technologies using VoIP (Voice over Internet Protocol); or through videoconferencing. They share by posting animations, digital art, photos, sound recordings, and videos. Online communities also promote a sense of shared identity and, whether subtly or explicitly, articulate norms and hierarchies that impart a sense of structure and order. Inevitably, however, the medium matters, affecting the nature and quality of online encounters and thus shaping the members' sense of community. Whether the results are constraining or liberating, frustrating or exhilarating depends on the users, their identities, and their circumstances. Just as some might find interacting online difficult because of language fluency or the strength of their Internet connection, others who are excluded from nonvirtual communities because of disability or prejudice might thrive best online.

Musical communities have existed online since the 1990s, an early example of which is the mod scene. A community of electronic music composers, both professional and amateur, the mod scene has for decades created a sense of belonging and connection among its members, most of whom have never encountered each other in the physical world.

Introduced by the US manufacturer Commodore in 1985, the Amiga was a family of personal computers that enjoyed modest popularity in Europe and the United States until it was discontinued in 1996. There would be little reason to mention the Amiga in a discussion of online musical community were it not for a software program called Ultimate Soundtracker. Created in 1987 by German software developer and composer Karsten Obarski, Soundtracker—best known by its shortened name—was originally a tool to create video game sounds and music for the Amiga. Obarski's innovation was to create a graphical interface that visually represented the four channels available on the Amiga's sound chip, allowing users to manipulate a sound's parameters and to create loops without having to write code. Soundtracker made computer music composition more broadly accessible, both because nonprogrammers could use it and because it could be used on personal computers. In 1988, Soundtracker itself became much more accessible when a Dutch programmer known as Exterminator modified it so that it could be used independent of the Amiga and then shared it free of charge. Further development led to the creation of the module file format that allowed users to easily save and distribute their creations.

Compositions using Soundtracker were known as modules, and then simply mods, and composers of mods came to be called trackers. Mods do not belong to any one genre, but they are all electronic and nearly all instrumental music, often in 4/4 meter with a steady beat; some of the most common genre classifications that the trackers themselves use are ambient, drum and bass, dance, techno, trance, and synthpop. Mods belong to the broader category of "chiptune," music originally created using sound chips manufactured for video games in the 1980s. The limited sound palette and compositional capabilities of these chips is an important feature of the chiptune aesthetic. Composers embrace these limitations; their works are judged by how well they rise to the challenge. A musical community of trackers emerged in the 1990s around the practice of sharing mods over the Internet; the mod scene, as its members call it, has remained active decades after the tools that launched it became obsolete.

Although most trackers rarely engage with each other in person, their interactions can generate a meaningful sense of community. Above all, an ethos of sharing and mutual support guides activities in the mod scene. Trackers exchange freely, allowing others to reuse parts of their compositions in their own tracks without charge. They workshop each other's music and offer praise, constructive feedback, and technical guidance. At the same time, there are clear norms that community members are expected to follow, and noncompliance has serious consequences.

Perhaps the strongest and most fraught set of norms center on ripping, the act of using material from another's track in one's own. Trackers often sample notes, melodies, or loops that they admire and then incorporate them into their own music, usually transforming them in some way. For many trackers, this is an essential part of their learning and creative processes. As long as certain criteria are met—the composer of the sample is credited and the sample is not considered too long or substantial—the practice is acceptable. No money needs to change hands and permission is not necessary. But ripping becomes a grave, norm-shattering act when one reuses another's track in large part or in whole with few, if any, modifications. In the mod scene such transgressions can lead to public shaming as well as the harshest punishment meted out by any community: banishment. The Mod Archive—a site that holds a massive collection of mods, provides an artist directory, hosts forums, and posts mod-related news— maintains a "Hall of Shame." The hall names rippers, cites the original song and composer, and identifies the nature of the plagiarism. The disgracing and expulsion of trackers help establish and enforce norms in the community.

The mod scene can justifiably be called a community. It is a durable social unit with a strong sense of identity, norms, and purpose accepted by its members. *Community*, however, is a loosely used term in Internet discussions, often invoked in connection with any website that allows users to share content or post comments. Many sites and platforms do promote sharing and communication around music, but seldom do these interactions lead to the kind of norms, relationships, and structures that define community. Beginning in the first decade of the 2000s, online platforms came to prominence that promoted social interactions on a vaster scale than had ever been seen before. An important early example was Myspace. Between 2005 and 2008, Myspace was the largest social networking site in the world, serving more than 100 million users each month. During this time, it became one of the major distributors of music; in its heyday millions of artists shared tens of millions of songs. Myspace was effective in allowing musicians to communicate directly with listeners, and many established devoted fanbases and launched significant careers through the site.

The social networking site Facebook, created in 2004, and YouTube, a video-sharing platform established in 2005, eventually displaced Myspace. They were later joined by other widely used services, including the Russian social network VK in 2006; Instagram, the US photo- and video-sharing app in 2010; and the Chinese video-sharing site TikTok (known domestically as Douyin) in 2016. Each of these has built global audiences in the hundreds of millions or billions, and although none of them focuses solely on music, all host music content and allow music-related discussion. Certain platforms also permit users to curate content around an artist, genre, or practice, whether as listeners, performers, composers, educators, scholars, sound engineers, or instrument builders. Some of these groups cater to narrow niches of the music world—Texas fans of Finnish folk metal, middle-aged scratch DJs, London-based wedding bands that specialize in North African gnawa music (all examples found on Facebook)—while others amass tens of thousands or even millions of members who celebrate their love for, say, bhangra, country music, hip hop, or K-pop. Regardless of their differences and intended audiences, they all aim to promote social interactions around music and have come to wield immense influence in musical culture and industry.

The major music streaming services of the early twenty-first century—Pandora (established in 2000 in the United States), Spotify (2006, Sweden), SoundCloud (2007, Sweden), iHeartRadio (United States, 2008), and Apple Music (United States, 2015)—have also fostered social interaction in a variety of ways. Spotify, for example, has sought to promote community for both artists and listeners. One section of the site, Spotify for Artists, was established to advise musicians on how to promote themselves more effectively, and offers interviews with successful artists and an analytics tool for understanding listener engagement. But creating community does not seem to be the primary goal; rather, it is part of a broader enterprise of career building and artistic development.

In 2016, Spotify announced a new hashtag to unify certain collections of songs, or playlists. The hashtag, #PressPlayForPride, was attached to playlists that promoted the dignity, rights, and visibility of LGBTQ people. Some playlists celebrated Pride Month, when parades and parties honor milestones in the history of LGBTQ struggles for equality. Others commemorated the horrific 2016 Pulse nightclub massacre in Florida, celebrated gay gym culture, or collected songs considered queer anthems. In some ways, these playlists replicated the ethos and atmosphere of spaces that brought together the LGBTQ community through music and technology. Disco—first as a type of nightclub and then as a music genre—has since the early 1970s served as a space and means to celebrate queer identity and solidarity, to challenge heteronormative conformity. Just as DJs curated sets of songs as a form of artistic expression and as a way to cater to nightclub audiences, so too have Spotify staffers and users curated playlists to express themselves and appeal to far-flung listeners.

LGBTQ playlists have only multiplied over the years on Spotify and connect to an array of identities, genres, themes, subjects, languages, and locations. In addition to the playlists, Spotify features a section on its site called Community, essentially a discussion forum, which was added to the service in 2012. But to what extent can a massive online platform, guided not just by human curators but also significantly by algorithms, serve community or act as a community? Spotify users engage with each other around LGBTQ subjects and queer-themed playlists, and the platform has made an effort to spotlight queer artists, but it would be hard to say that communities have arisen out of these interactions and initiatives. Moreover, some have criticized #PressPlayForPride as an exploitative commodification of oppressed minorities and point to the miniscule amount of money that goes to most of the artists on those playlists. These diverse views highlight the powerful connection between music and identity and remind us that no technology is fundamentally utopian or dystopian.

Music technologies have allowed people to connect in countless ways. Occasionally, robust, full-fledged communities grow around such technologies. More often, but no less significant, they catalyze gatherings, spur new forms of socializing or resuscitate moribund ones, shape existing hierarchies, tweak or reinforce norms, and bring physically distant people together around shared interests and identities.

In the spring of 2020, music began to fall silent around the world. Opera companies and symphony orchestras and pop groups canceled their concerts and tours. Community and church choirs stopped meeting. School marching bands marched no more. Karaoke bars and nightclubs closed their doors. Millions of ticket holders, if they were fortunate, received refunds for performances they could no longer attend. The loss to artists and audiences and the broader music industry—financially, creatively, psychologically—was immediate and devastating. But 2020, the year the coronavirus pandemic was born, was not the year the music died. Generations of technological advancements—radios and CD players, headphones and earbuds, portable players and digital files, streaming platforms and video-sharing sites—made it possible for billions around the world to listen to music without coming into contact with others. And yet, given the ease of consuming music in isolation, people went to great lengths during the pandemic to connect with each other through music. They did this through virtual choirs, Internet DJ parties and rap battles, online open-mic nights, long-distance jams, and many other ways. A time of social distancing, the pandemic only reinforced the fact that technology can be a powerful tool for fostering interaction and a means to meet our deep-seated need for musical, human connection.

Chapter 6
Noise

Noise—typically defined as unwanted sound—is an inevitably subjective matter. Ethnomusicologist Anthony Seeger discovered this when he recorded the music of the Kĩsêdjê people (previously known as Suyá) of Mato Grosso, Brazil, in 1982. Using a directional microphone, Seeger captured only the singing of the older men of the community, largely avoiding the shouting, laughing, and simulated bird calls of the boys and younger men in attendance, which he considered extraneous. The Kĩsêdjê were disappointed when Seeger played the tape for them. It did not capture the beauty and joy of the performance, they said, and left out essential parts of the music, what Seeger had at first considered crowd noise. When the Kĩsêdjê later obtained their own audio equipment, the recordings they made sounded quite different, reflecting their distinctive understanding of what counts as music and what counts as noise.

I made a similar assumption about what counts as noise the first time I heard an mbira, a Zimbabwean instrument with two rows of tuned metal keys, or tines. I was distracted by the buzzing sound that came from the vibration of bottle caps loosely affixed to the mbira's wooden base. Perhaps if the caps were tightened, I thought, the noise would disappear, allowing the "pure" tones of the mbira's metal keys to resound. But the very function of the bottle caps is to rattle in response to the vibrations of the keys.

What I heard as noise is in fact an integral part of the instrument's sound; without that sound the mbira is considered incomplete. We do not have to travel far from home to encounter divergent conceptions of music and noise. There are generational differences, as when parents tell children listening to their favorite music, "Turn off that noise!" Genre also plays an important role in determining whether a sound is music or noise. Consider the electric guitar. In heavy metal, the squealing of feedback and the growling of distortion are prized sounds, essential to the music. Within jazz, however, these are typically unwanted and disruptive—noises. Electric guitarists in these genres use distinctive techniques, technologies, and types of instruments either to cultivate or to avoid these sounds.

Defining noise as unwanted sound does not fully capture its complexity and significance. Noise is an inextricable and, in fact, valuable part of music. Every form of music making generates noise. These sounds cannot be eliminated entirely and serve valuable functions. The sharp intake of breath can intensify a vocal line; the clicking of saxophone keys offers clues about the mechanics of the instrument; the thwack of a plucked metal string against the wooden fingerboard of a double bass conveys its materiality and the effort of its player. These noises also help listeners distinguish one instrument from others, especially when we listen to recordings. When we cannot see the source of the sound, noises can flesh out the music disembodied by the medium.

Every recording and playback medium has its own characteristic set of noises as well. Phonographs crackle and whoosh as the needle (or stylus) moves through the disc's grooves; radios generate static; magnetic tape whirs when it speeds forward or backward and hisses during playback; CD players produce a high-pitched thrum as the disc rotates; the watery sound of low-bit-rate MP3s is distinctive to its medium. One can distinguish between 78 rpm shellac discs and 33⅓ rpm vinyl LPs

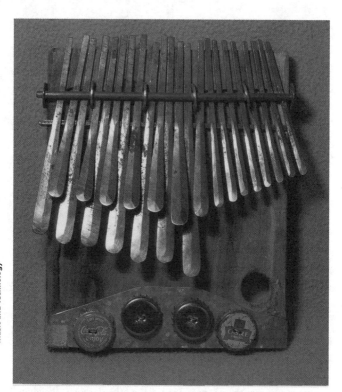

9. The mbira is a Zimbabwean instrument with tuned metal tines.
When the tines are played (pressed with the thumbs), the bottle caps
vibrate, creating a sound that is integral to the instrument's sonic
profile. This instrument is by Zimbabwean mbira maker and player
Tirivangani Chiongotere.

based on the noise they generate; the hum of a rewinding
reel-to-reel tape player sounds different from that of a cassette
tape. Videos capturing the noises of these media abound on the
Internet. A popular four-second recording called "Cassette Play
Sound Effect" consists solely of a cassette being inserted into a
machine and the play button being depressed. Such sounds are
often incorporated into audio recordings and films to evoke the

associated technologies and transport listeners to a different era. When these sounds are sought out and reproduced, they are no longer unwanted.

In 2000, the Argentine experimental music group Reynols released *Blank Tapes*, which features the sound of cassette tapes of varying vintage playing, unencumbered by anything recorded onto them. The fifty-minute album (released on CD) offers a sonic palette never meant to be heard. There is a technical term for the collective sounds generated by a medium that are not considered part of its signal: noise floor. The term recognizes that though the noises can be reduced, they cannot be reduced to zero. The word *floor* is telling, because it denotes a low or the lowest point in a structure. In "noise floor," it is typically used in a negative sense. At the same time, a floor is a vital part of any structure, something on which all else rests. Because the sounds that constitute a noise floor cannot be eliminated, they are by definition integral to that medium. Perhaps, then, we should hear these pops and clicks, static and crackles not as unwanted noises but as music, the native music of these technologies.

All sounds can be measured objectively in terms of pressure level, frequency, and so on, but whether they are considered music or noise is unavoidably subjective. What strikes one listener as extraneous is embraced by another as essential. Whole genres are sometimes regarded as noise by listeners unfamiliar with or antipathetic toward the music. When someone criticizes a form of music as noise, they are often judging the people who make or listen to it. Noise is determined by aesthetic, cultural, and personal values. To study noise is to examine these values, so often assumed and unarticulated.

Noise as music

The music/noise dichotomy has never been razor-sharp; musicians have been debating it for centuries. Consider the bullroarer, an instrument that dates to the Paleolithic era. Perhaps best known as an Australian Aboriginal instrument, where it is called a *turndun*, it is found around the world. Among the Navajo, or Diné, of North America it is a *tsin ndi'ni'*, or "groaning stick." The ancient Greeks called it a *rhombus*, which literally means "rumbling" or "whirling." When the etymologies of its many names are known, they usually refer to noises. Consisting of a wooden slat attached to a cord that is swung horizontally in a wide circle, it generates a variety of groaning, roaring, rumbling, and whirring sounds. The bullroarer has been used as a communication device, a tool in sacred rituals for invoking ancestors or warding off evil, and a musical instrument. Even when it is used in a specifically musical context, it retains its fundamental noisiness—it is heard as a noisemaker. Is its sound noise or is it music? It seems to be both simultaneously.

Noise, as the bullroarer tells us, has been a part of music since ancient times. In Western art music, composers have long sought to imitate the noises of the world in their instrumental and vocal works. Music that depicts the noises of war—firing cannons, clashing swords, galloping horses, and the like—was common in the 1500s and 1600s. Better-known examples include the 1555 vocal piece *La Guerre* ("The War"), by French composer Clément Janequin, and the *Battalia à 10* ("Battle for 10"), an instrumental piece from 1673 by Heinrich Biber of Germany. Perhaps the most famous piece of European battle music came from Russia—Pyotr Ilyich Tchaikovsky's 1880 orchestral work, *1812 Overture*, which in many performances employs actual cannons. Composers have also sought to imitate the noises of nature, as Antonio Vivaldi did in his set of violin concertos, *The Four Seasons* (ca. 1717), which mimics the barking, buzzing, and chirping of dogs, insects, and birds. Multiplying Vivaldi's seasons by three, Fanny Mendelssohn composed *Das Jahr* (The year, 1841), a collection of twelve piano pieces that suggest the sounds of nature as they unfold over the months of a year.

With the twentieth century came a profusion of pieces by classical music composers seeking to capture the cacophony of the machine age, often imitating the sounds of modern technologies. The Italian futurist artist Luigi Russolo made this connection between music, noise, and technology explicit in his 1913 manifesto, *L'Arte dei rumori* (The art of noises): "As it grows ever more complicated today, musical art seeks out combinations more dissonant, stranger, and harsher for the ear. Thus, it comes ever closer to noise-sound. This evolution of music is comparable to the multiplication of machines." Works such as *Suicide in an Airplane* (1916), a piano piece by US artist Leo Ornstein, and *The Iron Foundry* (1927), an orchestral work by the Soviet composer Alexander Mosolov, deploy relentless ostinatos (short, repeated phrases) and clashing dissonance both to render noises into music and to convey the fear and awe that these technologies aroused.

Composers and performers have also looked beyond traditional instruments and techniques to depict and create noise. Russolo spent more than fifteen years building a variety of acoustic instruments—assemblages of drums, strings, and megaphone-like horns—that he collectively called *intonarumori*, or noise intoners. Some composers conscripted nonmusical devices into musical service; *Ballet mécanique* (1924), by the US composer George Antheil, calls for an ensemble that includes electric bells, propellers, and sirens. Others looked to sound recording media to explore and blur the border between noise and music. In *Cinq études de bruits*—Five Noise Etudes—French composer and sound engineer Pierre Schaeffer recorded a variety of sounds, many of nonmusical objects such as boats and trains, cookware and toys, and then manipulated and arranged them into short studies that he presented in a Concert of Noises in 1948. These works used phonographs and records as their medium, but he soon embraced magnetic tape, which was becoming more widely available. He started calling his work *musique concrète*, the "concrete" pointing to the real-world sounds that he used as source material. At about the same time, the US composer John Cage was developing what he described as "tape music," a clear acknowledgment that these compositions were created with and not simply disseminated through a recording medium. Like Schaeffer, he collected and manipulated a variety of nonmusical sounds (and some musical sources), but Cage's approach was distinctive in his embrace of chance procedures. His philosophy was to "let sounds be sounds." In *Williams Mix* (1951–53), Cage developed a system that allowed sound sources and sonic parameters to be dictated by consulting the ancient Chinese text the *I Ching*, or the *Book of Changes*. Over the course of four and a quarter minutes, croaking frogs, piano chords, human speech, and electronic signals all jostle for the listeners' attention. Its first performance in 1958 was met by a raucous, extended ovation, the crowd noise segueing seamlessly from Cage's mix but lasting many times longer than any single sound in the piece.

Since the mid-twentieth century, examples of music created by harnessing the noise of sound recording and reproduction media have proliferated. A striking category comes from the repurposing—what some might consider the abuse or misuse—of recording technology. Consider three examples from Japan, which for decades has been a center of what is broadly known as noise music. For a 1965 concert, composer Mieko Shiomi coated a record of Carl Maria von Weber's 1819 piece *Invitation to the Dance* with water-soluble glue. Her performance consisted of slowly wetting the record with a syringe; drop by drop, she washed the glue away, allowing the phonograph needle to move ever more freely through the grooves as Weber's lilting music emerged. The performance poses questions about the distinction between noise and music. When does the sound of the needle moving (or struggling to move) through the record's grooves change from noise to music? Can the transformation from noise to music ever be pinpointed? In foregrounding the sound of the needle, was she positing a distinctive phonographic type of music that then disappeared as Weber's waltz came into focus?

In the mid-1980s, Yasunao Tone started capturing the noise of the compact disc, then still a new technology. Seeking to override the precision and predictability of the CD player, he affixed pieces of transparent sticky tape to the mirrored underside of the discs. He found that if he pricked tiny holes in the tape, he could thwart the error correction software built into CD players. The resulting "errors" created new sounds and rhythms (often described as a musical stuttering), transforming the machine into a musical instrument. The title of his 1997 piece, *Solo for Wounded CD*, suggests that in rendering the medium imperfect and unpredictable, he humanized the technology, simultaneously making it vulnerable while imbuing it with creative ability.

A lanky, long-haired, black-clad man enters a small, mostly bare stage. After adjusting a microphone, he walks back to a large amplifier. It is difficult to see what he does to the amplifier, but soon waves of distortion pour from it. The man, known by his stage name, Masonna, then grabs the microphone, knocking over its stand. He darts around the stage in unpredictable spasms, punching and slashing the air, throwing himself on the ground again and again. The sound—which he controls with a microphone, a small handheld device connected to the amplifier, and several effects pedals on the floor—is similarly spasmodic, shifting in pitch, timbre, and reverberation, always at an earsplitting volume. After about three minutes, he leaves the stage, gesticulating wildly and throwing himself down one final time. The crowd at this 2002 concert in Osaka cheers and applauds. Although Masonna's approach puts him in the same experimental tradition as Mieko Shiomi and Yasunao Tone, his work is part of a more recent scene and artistic practice known as *Japanoizu*, or Japanoise. Emerging around 1990, it is marked by extremely loud performances in which artists—sometimes known as noisicians—generate and manipulate feedback and distortion, often in aggressive or destructive ways. Performances typically require complex technological setups, and the painstaking assembly of the gear is regarded by initiated audience members as an important part of the experience, one that heightens the subsequent dismantling of the equipment.

The art of Mieko Shiomi, Yasunao Tone, and Masonna, though far from any mainstream musical practices, shares a common ambivalence about technology experienced in cultures around the world since the early part of the twentieth century. Shiomi and Tone were part of an international community known as Fluxus, a collective of experimental artists whose work, heavily influenced by John Cage, focused on process rather than product, always pushing boundaries and questioning received wisdom. Tone's work was also connected with a continent-crossing practice and genre that came to be known as glitch—the German group Oval is one of its most prominent practitioners—which uses the malfunctioning or refunctioning of recording technology as the primary source of its music. Japanoise may be most closely associated with Masonna's home country (and particularly Osaka), but noise bands proliferate around the world. The global engagement with noise spotlights both a broad fascination with technology and an abiding ambivalence and anxiety about its impact. Noise can represent violence and the loss of control and stand in for the destructive power of machines. To cultivate noise as an art form, then, is to exert control over technology, to humanize it, and to project, protect, and celebrate one's humanity in the process.

Noise as menace

The violent climax of the 1989 film *Do the Right Thing* turns on a dispute about the difference between noise and music. The confrontation centers on a large boom box as it blasts Public Enemy's hip hop track, "Fight the Power." To Radio Raheem, a young Black man and the owner of the boom box, "Fight the Power" is music. Sal, an older white man and the owner of the pizzeria where the scene is set, vehemently disagrees. "What did I tell ya 'bout dat noise?" Sal snarls. "Turn that JUNGLE MUSIC off. We ain't in Africa." Radio Raheem retorts, "This is music. My music." Then, according to the script, "Sal grabs his Mickey Mantle bat from underneath the counter and brings it down on Radio Raheem's box, again and again and again. The music stops." "My music!" Raheem cries in response to the destruction. The confrontation escalates, and by the end of the film Radio Raheem is dead, murdered by a police officer, and Sal's Pizzeria is in flames.

Do the Right Thing, though a work of fiction, reflects real-world attitudes about the links between music, noise, and violence. In the film, the music is hip hop, a genre that has been criticized as noisy and violent ever since it emerged as a form of popular culture in the late 1970s. The prominent US judge and legal scholar Robert Bork expressed a commonly held view when he condemned hip hop in 1996 as "little more than noise with a beat" and "violently obscene and brutal." Sentiments like these, which characterize a whole genre as debased and unworthy of being called music, are often expressed after only the most cursory encounters with its sound.

Technology plays a key role in these encounters, because those who denigrate hip hop most likely experience it through various media, whether cassettes, CDs, radio, video, or the Internet. Hip hop is made mobile through these technologies, meaning that some listeners' experience of the music—as with Sal and "Fight the Power"—is unsolicited and unwanted. Such contact tends to be fleeting, hardly permitting meaningful engagement with the music. But unwanted encounters, even if they lead listeners to condemn the music as noise, do not in themselves lead to violence. It is typically racism and other forms of identity-related animus that serve as the catalyst for such violence. A stark but by no means singular example of a technologically mediated encounter with hip hop that ended in murder is the 2012 shooting of an unarmed Black teenager, Jordan Davis, by a forty-five-year-old white man named Michael Dunn. Loud hip hop music, regarded by Dunn as a violent threat, was at the center of the ensuing trial. In fact, the case came to be known as the "Loud Music Trial."

On November 23, 2012, Dunn pulled into a gas station in Jacksonville, Florida, where Davis and three friends sat in a nearby car. Dunn could hear hip hop emanating from the teenagers' car stereo, later referring to it as "thumping noise," "thug music," and "rap crap." He confronted the boys, demanding that they turn off the music. They ultimately refused, and after an argument, Dunn retrieved a pistol from his car and shot at the vehicle. When the driver backed away evasively, Dunn continued to fire, ten times in all, with three bullets hitting Davis. Davis died from his wounds. Although none of the young men had weapons of any kind and although they sought to escape, Dunn claimed that he opened fire in self-defense. According to Dunn, Davis "had threatened my life" and became "louder and louder and more violent and more violent." Dunn seems to have transferred the volume and violence he perceived in the music to Davis. Given that Davis was younger, smaller, and unarmed, the true threat in this story was the racist white man with a gun. After two trials taking nearly two years, Dunn was convicted of murder. The killing of Jordan Davis was no anomaly. For as long as the music of African Americans has been played on recordings and broadcast over radio, certain listeners, many of them white, have condemned it as noise, invested it with violence, and believed it to be a threat to their safety. The power of technology to bring people together through music tends to be lauded as a good, and indeed it often is. But technologically facilitated musical encounters also shine a light on lurking animosities and entrenched inequities, sometimes with tragic consequences.

There is another type of musical encounter in which animosities and inequities are very much on the surface, where violence is in fact the intended outcome. This is the use of music in torture, especially as an outcome of state-sanctioned interrogations of prisoners of war. Music has been a torturer's tool for centuries.

Forced singing, where prisoners are humiliated and driven to exhaustion by being compelled to sing songs antithetical to their beliefs, is an old practice. But in the age of sound recording, and particularly with the development of digital recording technology in the 1980s and 1990s, musical torture has become more widely practiced. This came about because of the exploitation of the affordances of sound-reproducing technology, specifically its portability, manipulability, and repeatability. Recorded music is easily brought into any space where prisoners might languish and can be a permanent feature of interrogation rooms; its volume is readily controlled and can be set to earsplitting levels; with CDs and digital files, music can also be repeated for hours without requiring the intervention of the torturer. Music can facilitate what is known as "no-touch torture," but it is often no less harmful and degrading than any other form of brutalization. Digitally weaponized music, often coupled with flashing lights and hoods, forced nakedness, and stress positions, is used to disorient prisoners, deprive them of sleep, strip them of their sense of control, and instill extreme anxiety and dread. When such techniques have been documented, their nominal goal is to assist in interrogation, to facilitate the cooperation of enemies. They are, however, clearly a form of torture, which is defined by US law as conduct "specifically intended to inflict severe physical or mental pain or suffering."

The use of music in torture transforms what in one context may be beloved music into the most unwelcome, destructive noise. Consider documented examples of artists and music used by US interrogators during the so-called global war on terror in the first decade of the 2000s: Aerosmith, the Bee Gees, "I Love You" from *Barney and Friends*, Marilyn Manson, Meatloaf, Queen's "We Are the Champions," Britney Spears, and a variety of heavy metal and hip hop songs. Their use suggests that interrogators sought music that would be variously emasculating, feminizing, infantilizing, queerifying, or in some other way offensive to prisoners based on their culture or religion. Any music can become noise when played at excessive volumes and coupled with aggression, degradation, and deprivation. Music was regularly used by US interrogators in detention camps in Afghanistan, Cuba, Iran, Iraq, and a variety of undisclosed "dark prisons." Field manuals indicate that music was part of a broad interrogation approach known as *futility*, the goal of which was to convince detainees that resistance was in vain. An interrogation room at the US Air Force Base in Mosul, Iraq, outfitted with a strobe light and boom box, was known as "the disco." An army interrogator who questioned prisoners in "the disco" reported that he himself experienced anger, disorientation, and pain in his relentless use of music as noise. "Futility music" dehumanizes all involved.

The US military has authorized music as an appropriate means of obtaining information and cooperation in interrogations. Even if it is considered legal, we should worry about—and oppose—the weaponization of music. But we should not be surprised. Music and technology are tools, their value determined by those who wield them. When music is regarded as noise, it can also be heard and used as a form of menace, whether by listeners who interpret hip hop as a threat to their safety or by interrogators who blare heavy metal at prisoners.

Noise is inextricably connected with the tools and systems that create, reproduce, and disseminate sound. Whether in the form of instruments, recording gear, or playback equipment, music technology is inescapably noisy. Noise is not necessarily unwanted or extraneous. It can be gentle, nuanced, soothing, and beautiful. The noises that accompany the act of performance are informationally rich, enhancing the experience of the music we hear. The native noises of vinyl discs, magnetic tape, and CDs may form the basis of new works, performance practices, and genres. The mere existence of a robust market for noise-generating machines and apps designed as sleep aids makes it clear that listeners often embrace noise. The negative side of noise is the more familiar. Noise is meant to be abated, blocked, canceled, and dampened; vast amounts of money are spent every year on headphones and soundproofing in the endless quest to lower the sound floor. Noise can be a form of pollution. It is often regarded as ugly, offensive, or violent. To call someone's music noise is to reject their aesthetics, their values, and sometimes their humanity. Noise can be a threat and it can be a weapon.

To explore the connection between noise and technology is to discover the context-dependent nature of music. To return to the example of the mbira, I am far from the only Westerner to describe its sound as "buzzing," which suggests that it is something distinct, discrete, and thus removable from the mbira's music. *Buzzing* also has negative connotations, whether describing the unwelcome sound of insects or malfunctioning fluorescent light bulbs. Zimbabwean mbira players, however, discuss the instrument's sound very differently. In Shona, the language most closely associated with the mbira, there is no distinct word to describe the sound that outsiders hear as buzzing. In conception, language, and practice, it is not separable from the overall sonic profile of the instrument. This may seem like little more than interesting trivia, but conceptions of noise are often tied up with power relationships. A Zimbabwean mbira player once recalled how, during a recording session in London, a sound engineer insisted on taping down the bottle caps on his mbira to quiet the "noise." To the engineer this was an obvious remedy to a problem. But to silence the mbira's bottle caps was to exercise power over the player and impose foreign values that compromised the musician's artistic voice. Although the engineer may have seen this as an act of expediency and perhaps meant no offense, this silencing resonates with the kind of willful cultural ignorance that marked England's long and violent colonial rule in Zimbabwe, an era that, lasting until 1980, was likely within living memory of both engineer and player.

Glitch music offers another example of the complex power of noise. Glitch turns the typical valence of noise on its head but at the same time reinforces certain traditional social constructions. In glitch, technological malfunction and the noises that come from it are celebrated; noise becomes music, failure is defined as success. At the same time, glitch, like many technological realms, is dominated by men and masculinist language, leaving many women, transgender, and nonbinary musicians feeling alienated or excluded. Johanna Fateman and Kathleen Hanna, members of the US electronic rock group Le Tigre, noted a gendered double standard in the scene:

FATEMAN: It really struck us that, when men make mistakes, it's fetishized as glitch…

HANNA: Something beautiful.

FATEMAN: And when women do it, it's like…

HANNA: …a hideous mistake.

FATEMAN: Right, it's not considered an artistic innovation or statement or an intentional thing.

Other artists and scholars have also noted that discussions of glitch often celebrate masculine stereotypes. To note this, however, is not to single out glitch for censure; it simply reinforces the point that our engagement with technology reflects and enacts broader realities.

Noise, though commonly regarded as something to be avoided, minimized, or suppressed, is a richly expressive phenomenon. The noises of music technologies tell us a great deal about how music is made, what music means, how it has power, and how it reflects and shapes the world around us.

Chapter 7
Five theses about music and technology

Technology is not just a thing. It is also a way of talking and thinking about things. How we talk and think about technology affects how we experience, interpret, and seek to shape the world. Our understanding of the relationship between music and technology in turn influences how we value music and musicians, what we count as music, and whom we classify as musicians, all of which has real-world consequences. People are prepared to risk their own safety and willing to commit violence because of their musical beliefs and values, and music technologies have been at the center of life-and-death scenarios.

The stakes are rarely so extreme, but every day we make decisions about how to use our time, spend our money, and interact with others based on assumptions we make about music and technology. Often these assumptions suggest clear lines between the technological and the natural, between traditional musical instruments and playback devices, between live and recorded, between mediated and unmediated. In touting music as one of the great forces for good in the world we do not fully acknowledge the harm it may cause. We embrace clear cause-and-effect models of technological influence, missing the complexity of power relationships and cultural contexts that play out in the way we engage with music. In celebrating the achievements of inventors and innovators, we may overestimate their influence and neglect the agency and creativity of everyday users of technology. The assertions that follow are meant to challenge such assumptions, boundaries, and binaries. They are not stated as objective, enduring truths; rather, they are intended to provoke questions, prompt reflection, and encourage further exploration.

All music is technological

During a 1980 trip to Tokyo, US ethnomusicologist Charles Keil observed a variety of musical performances in his wanderings about the city: two older men singing in front of a shrine; a team of drummers accompanying dancers at a festival; street musicians performing for the opening of a supermarket; and amateurs singing in a neighborhood bar. Each case struck him as unusual, because all the musicians performed alongside recorded music, whether provided by a record player, tape deck, or karaoke machine. Seeing people singing or playing alongside machines felt wrong to him. Keil's reaction points to a dichotomy between the technological and natural (also expressed as between technology and art) common in many societies, particularly in the West. The two are often seen as fundamentally distinct categories. To this way of thinking, live music making is natural or artistic, while mechanically or electronically created and disseminated music is technological. But these are not distinct categories. Both describe human-made technologies used to transmit sound.

Another way to understand the dichotomy Keil experienced is as the opposition between live, or unmediated, music and recorded, or mediated, music. But all music, whether live or recorded, is mediated. In the simplest sense, a medium is a substance or space between two objects, and a medium always shapes or influences that which it mediates. Even if I sing to myself, the air around me and my own body mediate the sound. It is impossible to draw a clear line between the organic and the technological. We blur this line further when we incorporate the nonorganic into our bodies. Whether ear trumpets or hearing aids, cochlear implants or vibrotactile wearables, we have been challenging the distinction between the organic and the technological for centuries.

To insist that all music is technological is not to erase what is interesting, different, or remarkable about the variety of ways in which we create and experience music. In fact, it is quite the opposite. For example, some insist that live music is better than recorded music. In this view live music is authentic, spontaneous, and real, while recordings are artificial, manufactured, and cold. Others favor recorded music because it offers greater convenience and control, a haven from the distractions of noisy, uncomfortable venues. We can make equally adamant claims that our preferred mode of listening is the purer musical experience. But purism is a dead end, serving mostly to tout one's superiority, diminish the values of others, and limit rather than cultivate discussion and exchange. Live performances and sound recordings simply offer different ways of experiencing music. Recognizing both as technological and mediated allows us to identify and compare their distinctive affordances, limitations, and benefits. It empowers us to decide under what conditions we are better served by one or the other and to avail ourselves of a broader array of musical experiences.

Our relationship with music technology is fundamentally collaborative

Technology is often said to make our lives easier, to take care of work we once had no choice but to do. Consumer technologies— dishwashers, coffee makers, sewing machines, electric drills, and the like—are marketed as labor-saving devices. In reality, technology tends not to eliminate labor but to redistribute it or create the need for different kinds of labor. Work is still required to operate, clean, maintain, and repair these technologies. Music technologies are often conceived of in the same way, though "labor saving" has often been seen as a negative. In his 1906 article about then-new music technologies, "The Menace of Mechanical Music,"

John Philip Sousa proclaimed that "when music can be heard in the homes without the labor of study and close application, and without the slow process of acquiring a technic, it will be simply a question of time when the amateur disappears entirely." Ever since, a common critique of music technology is that it devalues the art precisely because it makes some aspect of it easier or unnecessary. This is a view we ought to resist because it obscures the fact that our relationship with music technology is fundamentally collaborative.

What is the difference between a traditional piano and the player piano? The most obvious distinction would seem to be that one requires a human to play it while the other plays itself. But the matter is not so simple. During its heyday at the turn of the twentieth century, most player pianos required humans to operate pedals and levers to add nuances of tempo, phrasing, and dynamics. These nuances made each performance unique; moreover, they demanded a skill set distinct from that needed to play the traditional piano. People even studied manuals and took lessons on how to become a good pianolist, a term popular among users of the technology. (*Pianola* was a common name for the instrument at the time.) The player piano is not, then, a technology that wholly eliminates human labor. Conversely, the traditional piano can be understood as a labor-saving technology. The sound of the piano is the sound of felt-covered wooden hammers striking wire strings. But pianists do not directly touch the strings or the hammers (at least not in the usual way of playing); this is done via a complex mechanism known as the piano's action. The action of a grand piano consists of twenty parts of varying sizes, shapes, and materials, and the pianist typically touches only one of them—the keys. The piano and player piano do not stand on opposite sides of a divide, where one side represents human-made music and the other machine-made music. They reside along a continuum, differing in the degree to which they distribute musical labor between player and instrument. All musical labor is in some way a collaboration between humans and the technologies they engage.

A twenty-first-century example of the technologically collaborative nature of music making is the video game *Guitar Hero*. First released in 2005, *Guitar Hero* employs a modified instrument that, like the pianola, divides the musical labor with the player. Holding the plastic, guitar-shaped controller, the player presses buttons on the fretboard to activate pitches in a prerecorded popular song; hitting the right buttons at the right time results in the full and correct melody. As with the player piano, *Guitar Hero* and its sequels, as well as games like *Rock Band* (2007) and *DJ Hero* (2009), enable collaborative musical activity. Critics have decried these video games as a poor substitute for "real" music making, and certainly, there are differences between playing *Guitar Hero* and playing a guitar. But the differences do not render one music making and the other patently not. Rather, game controllers and traditional instruments realize different forms of musical co-laboring, of collaboration.

A final comparison, this time between two traditional musical instruments, reinforces the continuum model of musical labor. With the pipe organ, a massive and complex instrument, players remotely operate a set of stops, keys, and pedals that generate sound with mechanical and often electrical assistance. On organs with mechanical action, that is, unassisted by electricity, the console where the player sits can be sixty-five feet, or more than twenty meters, from the pipes, where the sound comes out. Compare organ playing to hand drumming—where the performer's body makes direct contact with the sounding surface of the instrument. Are we willing to say that these are categorically different, that one is less "authentic" than the other because it technologically assisted? Probably not. And if we accept that playing the pipe organ is an act of music making, can we say that playing a pianola or *Guitar Hero* is self-evidently *not*? Trying to demarcate hard boundaries in these cases is a losing proposition. Rather than labor to defend rigid hierarchies we should instead seek commonalities among the vast possibilities of musical creation.

All uses of musical technologies reveal power relationships

On August 31, 1939, the *New York Times* published a one-sentence article: "Nazi Radio Says It with Music." The entire piece reads, "Each German news broadcast, with its reports of Polish 'chauvinism' and alleged atrocities 'against German nationals' begins and ends with a stirring martial tune called 'The March of the Germans in Poland.'" The next day, September 1, Germany invaded Poland, initiating World War II. This song and the broadcasts it bookended were one piece of a national strategy dating to the beginning of the Nazi regime. In its first year in power, 1933, the Reich released the *Volksempfänger*, the "people's receiver," an inexpensive radio created at the request of Joseph Goebbels, one of Adolf Hitler's most devoted associates and the head of the Reich Ministry of Public Enlightenment and Propaganda, the agency that enforced Nazi ideology. The Nazis recognized the political value of the radio. This is obvious from the programming of music like "The March of the Germans in Poland" and print advertisements for the *Volksempfänger* such as the one announcing "All of Germany Listens to the Führer with the People's Receiver."

The Nazis embraced radio as a propaganda tool to whip up support for the regime's war effort and to justify the genocide that led to the systematic murder of six million Jews and many others. Radio helped the regime expand and direct its power over its citizens, allies, and enemies alike. Although an extreme case, the Nazi use of radio illustrates how power relations underlie, motivate, and are articulated by the manifold ways in which humans engage with music technologies. The exercise and flow of power in the use of music technology are dazzlingly varied, as are the lessons to be drawn. Nazi radio, as well as the US military's deployment of sound recordings as a form of torture in the early 2000s, demonstrates the vast scope of music's power when conscripted to serve reprehensible, state-sanctioned ends. At the same time, these examples undercut a solely utopian view of music.

The flow of power is neither predictable nor easily controlled, and there are striking cases in which music is deployed as a tool to subvert power structures. The US folk musician Woody Guthrie very directly used his voice to oppose the Nazi regime, writing songs denouncing, ridiculing, and threatening Adolf Hitler. Sometime in the early 1940s, he painted "This Machine Kills Fascists" on the side of his acoustic guitar. He had borrowed the phrase from factory workers manufacturing materiel for the war effort who wrote those words on their lathes and drill presses. For Guthrie, it seems, his guitar was likewise a tool in the war effort.

Often, music serves as a form of resistance in less explicit, but no less potent forms. This is true in the case of the harmonium in India and the accordion in Madagascar, when both instruments were modified to accommodate local musical practices and cultural values and in doing so served anticolonial impulses. There is also the steel drum, created on the Caribbean island of Trinidad. In 1883, the British colonial government, seeking to suppress the celebration of Carnival among the descendants of freed slaves, banned the use of animal skin drums. In response, Afro-Trinidadians developed an alternative form of percussion music that came to be known as Tamboo Bamboo, in which groups of players pound dried bamboo stalks of varying lengths and widths on the ground to create distinct pitches and timbres. In the 1930s, Tamboo Bamboo musicians started incorporating metal instruments into their ensembles, and late in that decade, the first steel drum, also known as pan or steelpan, was created.

However, it was the local response to another form of foreign occupation that led to the explosive growth of these instruments

10. Woody Guthrie plays his guitar with the label "This Machine Kills Fascists" in 1943. Guthrie wrote and performed many antifascist songs, particularly denouncing Adolf Hitler.

and ensembles. In 1940, the United States and the United Kingdom signed the destroyers-for-bases deal, in which the United States transferred fifty Navy destroyers to the United Kingdom in exchange for the rights to build military bases on several of its territories, including Trinidad. The proliferation of discarded fifty-five-gallon oil drums on the bases created an immediate and plentiful (if not willingly offered) supply of materials for Afro-Trinidadian instrument makers, who cut the cast-off containers into different sizes, and hammered them into pitched percussion instruments that were played marching band style with mallets.

These new instruments were not at first welcomed by the authorities; their music was denigrated as noise and police regularly confiscated them. Over time, however, steelpan came to be a musical and cultural symbol of the island and, with independence in 1962, the pride of the nation of Trinidad and Tobago. Those who had been formerly opposed or indifferent to the instrument embraced it. In 1957, the US military purchased sixteen instruments from Trinidadian steelpan makers and formed a Navy Steel Band that performed hundreds of concerts a year over the ensuing decades. Shell Oil Company, which had a significant presence on the island, sponsored one of Trinidad's most famous groups, the Invaders, which then became the Shell Invaders Steelband in 1960. Behind the melodious sounds of this now internationally beloved instrument and sonic signifier of a nation lies a long and complex set of power relations marked by oppression and occupation, resistance and invention, adoption and cooptation.

There is another lesson to be drawn from these examples. In perhaps every case in which a form of technology is used against its generally accepted purpose for musical ends, it can be understood as a means to exert control and express power. In the case of musical propaganda and torture, it is the oppressors wielding the technology. But it is usually only in such extreme cases that those in power subvert technological norms; typically they set those norms. More often, oppressed or marginalized peoples are the ones hacking or tweaking musical technologies. This was true of the musicians of India, Madagascar, and Trinidad who modified, repurposed, or created instruments. This was true of the African American and Black British youth of Houston and London who hacked their turntables to create new musical genres—chopped and screwed and drum and bass. Whether the music is meant to be aggressive or laid back, angry or joyous, these are acts of sonic resistance in the face of oppression.

The mass mediation of music has not eliminated cultural differences

Sometime in 1985, Zimbabwean brothers Akim and Dumisani Ndlovu saw a movie that changed their lives: *Beat Street*. Set in the South Bronx, New York, *Beat Street* celebrates the hip hop arts of the DJ, dancer, rapper, and graffiti writer. The brothers were most inspired by the dance scenes, returning to watch *Beat Street* again and again, then staging impromptu dance performances outside the Harare theater for exiting filmgoers. The hip hop the Ndlovus encountered in Zimbabwe was imported from the United States. They heard Run-DMC on cassette tape; they saw kids breaking (or breakdancing) on television during the closing ceremonies of the 1984 Olympics in Los Angeles. Most people around the world first experienced hip hop in electronically mediated form, whether through analog means in its early years or through digital streaming services, video-sharing platforms, or social media.

Because of the globalization and popularity of US hip hop, it is not surprising that many budding hip hop artists around the world learn by imitating American artists. But the globalization of hip hop has not led to homogeneity. When the Ndlovu brothers (known under their professional names, Akim Funk Buddha and Dumi Right) formed a rap duo, they celebrated their heritage and called themselves Zimbabwe Legit. Their 1991 song, "Doin' Damage in My Native Language," switches back and forth between English and Ndebele. Their music proudly asserts their African roots while simultaneously embracing US hip hop culture and practice, for example, sampling 1970s American funk and soul. Also in the early 1990s, members of the Palestinian group DAM learned to rap in part by imitating the English-language videos of popular US artists such as Tupac Shakur. They never lost their love of Tupac, but they began rapping in Arabic and addressed the experience of Arabic-speaking Palestinians growing up in Israel. For these artists and countless others around the world, hip hop may start as a US import, but it soon becomes a vehicle for regional languages, cultural practices, and musical traditions, a means to engage with local history and politics. Hip hop has also become a way to preserve and disseminate indigenous languages around the world, whether Cherokee in North Carolina, the Quechuan languages of the Peruvian Andes, or Sámi, spoken in the northern regions of Norway, Sweden, and Finland. Such cases represent a rich dynamic, in which a cultural commodity exported by a global superpower is used to resist the effects of commodification and globalization on endangered cultures.

Hip hop offers just one example of what is known as glocalization, a process in which imported products or practices are transformed as they become incorporated into new contexts, but still maintain aspects of their original identity. The flow of glocalized culture does not always originate in the West. Karaoke started as an identifiably Japanese import in Britain, but later became as British as sing-alongs in corner pubs. Another example is K-pop, part of what is known as *Hallyu*, or the Korean wave. The music, dancing, and fashion that exemplify K-pop were initially influenced by teen-oriented US pop music trends and hip hop dance moves in the 1990s; over time, it became an identifiably Korean cultural product and global phenomenon devotedly consumed by non-Korean fans. In late 2020, "Life Goes On" by BTS made history in the United States by becoming the first Korean-language song to reach number one on the Billboard Hot 100 chart. Korean popular culture has become influential among young people in the United States; they listen to K-pop, imitate the fashion and recreate the choreography of their favorite "idols," watch Korean television shows (known as K-dramas), and study the language. But as is happening elsewhere in the world, K-pop will likely come to take on regional accents and practices in the United States as it is further adopted into local culture.

The examples of hip hop, karaoke, and K-pop challenge any simple model of technological influence. The complexity of cultural flows in which global and local forces simultaneously shape music creation and consumption and the sheer unpredictability of taste and trends expose the flaws in deterministic thinking about technology. When algorithms seem to tell us what we want and recommendation systems exploit the neuroscience of addiction to encourage binge consumption, the idea that technology directly determines our tastes or actions may seem compelling. But technological determinism minimizes key forces that shape our musical experience more deeply than any feature of technology: personal agency and culture. If we are to understand music technology we must fully account for the people who use it, their histories and traditions, their drive to express themselves and find meaning in the world.

The study of music technology is the study of people

The study of technology would seem to be a study of machines and systems. And, of course, it is. When we study music technology, we examine the affordances and interfaces of the phonograph and radio, magnetic tape and synthesizers, file-sharing and digital streaming platforms. But just as the obvious objects of technological study are not the only important ones—instruments and notation should also be taken seriously as technologies—the most significant objects of this study are not objects at all, but people. Popular histories of technology do in fact focus on people. They often celebrate inventors and innovators, the larger-than-life figures whose brilliance, determination, and vision are said to change the lives of millions and alter the course of history. These people matter, but they have come to matter too much. They tend to represent a narrow segment of the population: they are typically men, often white, and usually come from the world's richest nations. A more expansive view acknowledges the contributions of technologists

110

who do not look like those in the pantheon, but also the much larger population of everyday users and consumers of technology.

Take the example of the musical handclapping and rope-jumping games of African American girls. From a traditional view, these would not be regarded as technological practices. There is nothing obviously technological about clapping hands and jumping rope. But the perspective changes when we accept the human body as a form of technology and define music technology as any tool or system designed or used to facilitate the creation, preservation, reception, or dissemination of music. In her book *The Games Black Girls Play*, ethnomusicologist Kyra Gaunt puts it plainly: "The body is a technology of black musical communication and identity." The purpose of considering these games as technological is not to "elevate" handclapping and rope jumping or to diminish any other practices, but to insist that they be taken seriously and to see them as belonging to a broad spectrum of music-technological practice. Accepting this wider view of technology prompts provocative, productive questions we might not have thought to ask. Why are handclapping and rope jumping games not deemed technological? Because they do not use what is conventionally understood as technology? Because they are games played by Black girls? The fact that the answer to both questions is yes ought to lead us to rethink our assumptions.

The study of technology should be the study of people—all the people—who create and use technology. The study of *music* and technology should be the study of how and why people engage with, conceive of, adopt, and adapt to technology as they create and experience music. It should seek to understand how our use of music technology expresses and shapes our identities, cultures, and politics. It should plumb and illuminate all the ways in which we develop and deploy tools to satisfy the ancient and ongoing human need for connection through music.

References

Chapter 1: Music as technology

Voltaire's dismissal of the piano is quoted in Edwin M. Good, *Giraffes, Black Dragons, and Other Pianos: A Technological History of Cristofori to the Modern Concert Grand* (Stanford, CA: Stanford University Press, 1982), 1.

Sousa declared his views on technology in John Philip Sousa, "The Menace of Mechanical Music," *Appleton's* 8 (1906): 278–84.

Dolly Parton's designation of her fingernails as musical instruments is reported in Emily Kirkpatrick, "Dolly Parton Explains Why Her Acrylic Nails Are Credited as a Musical Instrument on Her Album," *Vanity Fair*, October 13, 2020, https://www.vanityfair.com/style/2020/10/dolly-parton-nails-9-to-5-graham-norton-show.

The Paleolithic flute is described in Nicholas J. Conard, Maria Malina, and Susanne C. Münzel, "New Flutes Document the Earliest Musical Tradition in Southwestern Germany," *Nature* 460 (August 6, 2009): 737–40.

Debates about Auto-Tune in gospel music are found in the blog post (and accompanying reader commentary), "Auto-Tune and Gospel Music Don't Go Together!" *The Old Black Church* (blog), April 30, 2010, https://theoldblackchurch.blogspot.com/2010/04/auto-tune-and-gospel-music-dont-go.html.

The reception of the harmonium in India is discussed in Matt Rahaim, "That Ban(e) of Indian Music: Hearing Politics in the Harmonium," *Journal of Asian Studies* 70 (August 2011): 657–82. For the reclassification of the harmonium, see "No GST on Sitar, but Tax String on Guitar," *Times of India*, September 11, 2017,

http://timesofindia.indiatimes.com/business/india-business/
no-gst-on-sitar-but-tax-string-on-guitar/articleshow-
print/60454903.cms. For the list of exempted instruments, see
pages 5–7 of "List of Goods for Change in GST Rate Recommended
by GST Council in Its 21st Meeting Held on 9th September, 2017"
(Hyderabad, India: India Goods and Service Tax Council, 2017),
http://texmin.nic.in/sites/default/files/changedGSTrates21stGST-
meeting.pdf.

The examples of technological determinism come from Sousa,
"The Menace of Mechanical Music," and Michael Hann,
"How Spotify's Algorithms Are Ruining Music," *Financial
Times*, May 2, 2019, https://www.ft.com/content/
dca07c32-6844-11e9-b809-6f0d2f5705f6.

The technological utopian examples come from "New Remedy for
Deafness: Dr. Leech Believes That the Phonograph Will Cause a
Cure," *New York Times*, May 23, 1892, 8; Evan O'Neill Kane,
"Phonograph in Operating Room," *Journal of the American
Medical Association* 62 (June 1914): 1829; Horace Johnson,
"Department of Recorded Music: Phonographs in the Home,"
Etude, February 1922, 88; and Janelle Brown, "The Jukebox
Manifesto," *Salon*, November 13, 2000, http://www.salon.
com/2000/11/13/jukebox/.

The adoption and adaptation of the accordion in Madagascar is
discussed in Ron Emoff, *Recollecting from the Past: Musical
Practice and Spirit Possession on the East Coast of Madagascar*
(Middletown, CT: Wesleyan University Press, 2002), 96–104.

Chapter 2: Bodies and senses

Helen Keller's account of Beethoven on the radio was first published
as "Helen Keller Gets Music by Radio," *New York Times*, February 10,
1924, S6. The article is reprinted, with commentary, in
Timothy D. Taylor, Mark Katz, and Tony Grajeda, eds., *Music,
Sound, and Technology in America: A Documentary History of
Early Phonograph, Cinema, and Radio* (Durham, NC: Duke
University Press, 2012), 271–22.

The animation that demonstrates the phenomenon of visually evoked
auditory response was posted by Lisa DeBruine at https://twitter.
com/LisaDeBruine/status/937105553968566272, December 2,
2017.

Bradley Kincaid is quoted in Kristine McCusker, "'Dear Radio Friend': Listener Mail and the *National Barn Dance*, 1931–1941," *American Studies* 39 (Summer 1998): 173–95.

Al Jarvis is quoted in Laurence W. Etling, "Al Jarvis: Pioneer Disc Jockey," *Popular Music & Society* 23 (1999): 41–52.

Evelyn Glennie explains how she hears with her whole body in "Hearing Essay," *Evelyn Glennie: Teaching the World to Listen*, January 1, 2015, https://www.evelyn.co.uk/hearing-essay/.

A contemporaneous review of a musical android performance is "Musical Chit-Chat," *Dwight's Journal of Music*, March 29, 1856, 205.

K-pop holograms are discussed in Suk-Young Kim, *K-Pop Live: Fans, Idols, and Multimedia Performance* (Stanford University Press, 2018), 129–60.

Chapter 3: Time

The patent that discusses what came to be known as a click track is W. E. Disney et al., Method and apparatus for synchronizing photoplays, US Patent 1,941,341, filed April 2, 1931, and issued December 26, 1933. The patent can be seen at https://patents.google.com/patent/US1941341A/en.

The research on tempo trends in twentieth-century pop music is reported in Stephen F. Roessner, "The Beat Goes Static: A Tempo Analysis of U.S. Billboard Hot 100 #1 Songs from 1955–2015," *Audio Engineering Society Convention*, Paper 9849, October 8, 2017.

Ravi Shankar's remarks about the challenges of playing for different media come from a 1965 interview by Carl Wildman, "Talking About Music: East Comes West," quoted in David VanderHamm, "The Social Construction of Virtuosity: Musical Labor and the Valuation of Skill in the Age of Electronic Media" (PhD diss., University of North Carolina at Chapel Hill, 2017), 234.

"U Smile (Slowed Down 800%)" is accessible at https://soundcloud.com/mesiuepiescha/justin-bieber-u-smile-slowed-down-800.

"9 Beet Stretch" can be heard at http://www.expandedfield.net.

The politics of Chopped and Screwed is explored in Aram Sinnreich and Samantha Dols, "Chopping Neoliberalism, Screwing the Industry: DJ Screw, the Dirty South, and the Temporal Politics of Resistance," in *Hip-Hop Theory: Time, Technology, and the 21st Century*, ed. Roy Christopher (Minneapolis: University of Minnesota Press, forthcoming).

Daphne Oram's remarks about the tape recorder come from *An Individual Note: Of Music, Sound and Electronics* (London: Galliard, 1972).

Steve Reich's remarks about *Come Out* are quoted in Andy Beta, "Blood and Echoes: The Story of *Come Out*, Steve Reich's Civil Rights Era Masterpiece," *Pitchfork*, April 28, 2016, http://pitchfork.com/features/article/9886-blood-and-echoes-the-story-of-come-out-steve-reichs-civil-rights-era-masterpiece/.

Chuck D.'s comments about looping are quoted in Mark Dery, "Public Enemy: Confrontation," *Keyboard* 16 (September 1990): 92.

KT Tunstall's 2010 live performance of "Black Horse & the Cherry Tree" is accessible at https://www.youtube.com/watch?v=T7oIaoL7joM.

Chapter 4: Space

The relationship between sound and cave art is proposed in Rupert Till, "Sound Archeology: Terminology, Paleolithic Cave Art and the Soundscape," *World Archaeology* 46 (2014): 292–304.

Architectural acoustics in St. Mark's Basilica is discussed in Deborah Howard and Laura Moretti, *Sound and Space in Renaissance Venice: Architecture, Music, Acoustics* (New Haven, CT: Yale University Press, 2009). The deleterious impact of tonic sol-fa in Zimbabwe is asserted in Mhoze Chikowero, *African Music, Power, and Being in Colonial Zimbabwe* (Bloomington: Indiana University Press, 2015).

"Outloud listening" is theorized in Sindhumathi Revuluri, "Stereos in the City: Moving through Music in South India," in *The Oxford Handbook of Mobile Music Studies*, vol. 2, ed. Sumanth Gopinath and Jason Stanyek (New York: Oxford University Press, 2014).

The phenomenon of "dancing grannies" in Hangzhou is discussed in Jing Wang, "Throbbing Crowds: Of Dancing Grannies and Acoustic Milieus in Contemporary China," *Social Science Information* 58 (2019): 377–89.

A history of X-ray records is told in Stephen Coates, *X-Ray Audio: The Strange Story of Soviet Music on the Bone* (London: Strange Attractor, 2015).

The workings of El Paquete Semanal are outlined in Michaelanne Dye, David Nemer, Josiah Mangiameli, Amy S. Bruckman, and Neha Kumar, "El Paquete Semanal: The Week's Internet in

Havana," in *Proceedings of the 2018 CHI Conference on Human Factors in Computing Systems*, paper 639, 2018.

Bhutan's record stamps are the subject of Chris May, "The Curious Tale of Bhutan's Playable Record Postage Stamps," *The Vinyl Factory*, December 30, 2015, https://thevinylfactory.com/features/the-curious-tale-of-bhutans-playable-record-postage-stamps/.

The official website dedicated to NASA's Golden Record is https://voyager.jpl.nasa.gov/golden-record/.

Chapter 5: Community

The sources for telephone concerts are "Grand Telephone Concert," Corinthian Hall, Rochester, NY, March 12, 1878, collection of the Sibley Music Library, Eastman School of Music; and "Prof. Gray's Telephone Concert: Successful Transmission of a Musical Performance from Philadelphia to New York," *New York Times*, April 3, 1877, 5.

Alice Talbot's phonograph gatherings in 1920s Maine are described in Alice Talbot, "The Development of a Musical Appreciation Class," *Phonograph Monthly Review* 3 (October 1928): 8–9, 12.

A history of *rajio taisō* is told in Kerim Yasar, *Electrified Voices: How the Telephone, Phonograph, and Radio Shaped Modern Japan, 1868–1945* (New York: Columbia University Press, 2018).

Research on karaoke in Brazil, Japan, and the United Kingdom is drawn from Torū Mitsui and Shūhei Hosokawa, eds., *Karaoke around the World: Global Technology, Local Singing* (London: Routledge), 1998, especially William H. Kelley, "The Adaptability of Karaoke in the United Kingdom," 83–101, and Shūhei Hosokawa, "Singing in a Cultural Enclave: Karaoke in a Japanese-Brazilian Community," 139–65; and Zhou Xun and Francesca Tarocco, *Karaoke: The Global Phenomenon* (London: Reaktion, 2007).

Information on the mod scene comes from René T. A. Lysloff, "Musical Community on the Internet: An On-line Ethnography," *Cultural Anthropology* 18 (2003): 233–63.

Chapter 6: Noise

The example of recording the Kīsêdjê comes from Anthony Seeger, *Why Suyá Sing: A Musical Anthropology of an Amazonian People* (Urbana, IL: University of Illinois Press), 77–78.

"Cassette Play Sound Effect" can be heard at https://www.youtube.com/watch?v=cpeuGKT8r2Q.

Mieko Shiomi's music is described in Sally Kawamura, "Appreciating the Incidental: Mieko Shiomi's 'Events,'" *Women & Performance: A Journal of Feminist Theory* 19 (2009): 311–36.

Masonna's performances of noise are discussed in David Novak, *Japanoise: Music at the Edge of Circulation* (Durham, NC: Duke University Press, 2013), 44–46; and the Masonna performance described in this chapter can be viewed on YouTube: "Masonna Festival beyond Innocence, Bridge, Osaka 2002 Japanoise," July 24, 2013, https://www.youtube.com/watch?v=ylDuOmEoZx0.

The second draft of the script of *Do the Right Thing*, dated March 1, 1988, can be found at The Internet Movie Script Database, https://imsdb.com/scripts/Do-The-Right-Thing.html.

Robert Bork expresses his criticism of hip hop in *Slouching towards Gomorrah: Liberalism and American Decline* (New York: Regan Books, 1996), 124, 135, and elsewhere. Quotations from the "Loud Music Trial" come from William Cheng, *Loving Music till It Hurts* (New York: Oxford University Press, 2020), 173–226.

The use of music and torture in the US global war on terror is the subject of Suzanne G. Cusick, "'You Are in a Place That Is out of the World . . .': Music in the Detention Camps of the 'Global War on Terror,'" *Journal of the Society for American Music* 2 (2008): 1–26.

The definition of torture in US law is codified in 8 U.S.C. §§ 2340–2340 A and can be found at https://www.justice.gov/file/18791/download.

The comments of Johanna Fateman and Kathleen Hanna about gender in the glitch music scene come from Tara Rodgers, *Pink Noises: Women on Electronic Music and Sound* (Durham, NC: Duke University Press, 2010), 249–50.

The story of the mbira player in London—Chartwell Dutiro—is mentioned in Merlyn Driver, "The Buzz Aesthetic and Mande Music: Acoustic Masks and the Technology of Enchantment," *African Music* 10 (2017): 95–118.

Chapter 7: Five theses about music and technology

Charles Keil describes his technological encounters in Tokyo in Charles Keil, "Music Mediated and Live in Japan," *Ethnomusicology* 28 (January 1984): 91–96.

The brief account of the song "The March of the Germans in Poland" is found in "Nazi Radio Says It with Music," *New York Times*, August 31, 1939, 2.

Research on the *Volksempfänger* is drawn from Brian Currid, *A National Acoustics: Music and Mass Publicity in Weimar and Nazi Germany* (Minneapolis: University of Minnesota Press, 2006).

The history of Trinidadian steelpan is chronicled in Kim Johnson, *From Tin Pan to TASPO: Steelband in Trinidad, 1939–1951* (Kingston, Jamaica: University of the West Indies Press, 2011).

The story of the Ndlovu brothers' introduction to hip hop is retold in Mark Katz, *Build: The Power of Hip Hop Diplomacy in a Divided World* (New York: Oxford University Press, 2019), 10–11.

The story of the hip hop group DAM is told in the 2008 film *Slingshot Hip Hop*, https://vimeo.com/195690477.

Kyra D. Gaunt discusses the Black body as a form of technology in *The Games Black Girls Play: Learning the Ropes from Double-Dutch to Hip-Hop* (New York: New York University Press, 2006), 59.

Further reading

Overviews, surveys, and collections

Greene, Paul D., and Thomas Porcello, eds. *Wired for Sound: Engineering and Technologies in Sonic Cultures*. Middletown, CT: Wesleyan University Press, 2004.

Katz, Mark, and Brian Jones. "Music and Technology." In *Oxford Bibliographies Online*, last modified June 27, 2018. https://www.oxfordbibliographies.com/view/document/obo-9780199757824/obo-9780199757824-0111.xml, 2018.

Pinch, Trevor, and Karin Bijsterveld, eds. *The Oxford Handbook of Sound Studies*. New York: Oxford University Press, 2012.

Taylor, Timothy D., Mark Katz, and Anthony Grajeda, eds. *Music, Sound, and Technology in America: A Documentary History of Early Phonograph, Cinema, and Radio*. Durham, NC: Duke University Press, 2012.

Bodies and senses

Birdsall, Carolyn, and Anthony Enns, eds. *Sonic Mediations: Body, Sound, Technology*. Newcastle, UK: Cambridge Scholars Press, 2008.

Eidsheim, Nina Sun, and Katherine Meizel, eds. *The Oxford Handbook of Voice Studies*. New York: Oxford University Press, 2019.

McLeod, Ken. "Living in the Immaterial World: Holograms and Spirituality in Recent Popular Music." *Popular Music and Society* 39 (2016): 501–15.

Papetti, Stefano, and Charalampos Saitis, eds. *Musical Haptics*. New York: Springer, 2018.

Stras, Laurie. "Subhuman or Superhuman? (Musical) Assistive Technology, Performance, Enhancement, and the Aesthetic/Moral Debate." In *The Oxford Handbook of Music and Disability Studies*, edited by Blake Howe, Stephanie Jensen-Moulton, Neil Lerner, and Joseph Straus, 176–90. New York: Oxford University Press, 2016.

Gender, race, and sexuality

Jarman-Ivens, Freya. *Queer Voices: Technologies, Vocalities, and the Musical Flaw*. London: Palgrave Macmillan, 2011.

Lewis, George E., ed. "Technology and Black Music in the Americas." Special issue, *Journal of the Society for American Music* 2 (May 2008).

Rodgers, Tara. *Pink Noises: Women on Electronic Music and Sound*. Durham, NC: Duke University Press, 2010.

Sewell, Amanda. *Wendy Carlos: A Biography*. New York: Oxford University Press, 2020.

Space

Born, Georgina, ed. *Music, Sound and the Reconfiguration of Public and Private Space*. Cambridge: Cambridge University Press, 2013.

Gopinath, Sumanth, and Jason Stanyek, eds. *The Oxford Handbook of Mobile Music Studies*. 2 vols. Oxford: Oxford University Press, 2014.

Howard, Deborah, and Laura Moretti. *Sound and Space in Renaissance Venice: Architecture, Music, Acoustics*. New Haven, CT: Yale University Press, 2009.

Thompson, Emily. *The Soundscape of Modernity: Architectural Acoustics and the Culture of Listening in America, 1900–1933*. Cambridge, MA: MIT Press, 2002.

Noise

Campos-Fonseca, Susan, and Julianne Graper. "Noise, Sonic Experimentation, and Interior Coloniality in Costa Rica." In *Experimentalisms in Practice: Music Perspectives from Latin America*, edited by Ana R. Alonso-Minutti, Eduardo Herrera, and

Alejandro L. Madrid, 161–85. New York: Oxford University Press, 2018.

Hegarty, Paul. *Noise/Music: A History*. New York: Continuum, 2007.

Thompson, Marie. *Beyond Unwanted Sound: Noise, Affect and Aesthetic Moralism*. New York: Bloomsbury, 2017.

Notation and printing

El-Mallah, Issam. *Arab Music and Musical Notation*. Tutzing, Germany: Hans Schnieder, 1997.

Jun-yon, Hwang, Kim Jin-Ah, and Lee Yong-Shik, eds. *Musical Notations of Korea*. Seoul: National Gugak Center, 2010.

Kelly, Thomas Forrest. *Capturing Music: The Story of Notation*. New York: W. W. Norton, 2015.

Automata and mechanical musical instruments

Bowers, Q. David. *Encyclopedia of Automatic Musical Instruments*. Vestal, NY: Vestal Press, 1972.

Miller, Kiri. "Schizophonic Performance: *Guitar Hero, Rock Band*, and Virtual Virtuosity." *Journal of the Society for American Music* 3, no. 4 (November 2009): 395–429.

Suisman, David. "Sound, Knowledge, and the 'Immanence of Human Failure': Rethinking Musical Mechanization through the Phonograph, the Player-Piano, and the Piano." *Social Text* 28, no. 1 (Spring 2010): 13–34.

Voskuhl, Adelheid. *Androids in the Enlightenment: Mechanics, Artisans, and Cultures of the Self*. Chicago: University of Chicago Press, 2013.

Electronic and computer music

Butler, Mark J. *Playing with Something That Runs: Technology, Improvisation, and Composition in DJ and Laptop Performance*. Oxford: Oxford University Press, 2014.

Dean, Roger T., ed. *The Oxford Handbook of Computer Music*. New York: Oxford University Press, 2009.

Holmes, Thom. *Electronic and Experimental Music: Technology, Music, and Culture*. 5th ed. New York: Routledge, 2016.

Recording

Bayley, Amanda, ed. *Recorded Music: Performance, Culture and Technology*. Cambridge: Cambridge University Press, 2010.

Cook, Nicholas, Eric Clarke, Daniel Leech-Wilkinson, and John Rink. *The Cambridge Companion to Recorded Music*. Cambridge: Cambridge University Press, 2009.

Katz, Mark. *Capturing Sound: How Technology Has Changed Music*. Rev. ed. Berkeley, CA: University of California Press, 2010.

Zagorski-Thomas, Simon, and Andrew Bourbon, eds. *The Bloomsbury Handbook of Music Production*. London: Bloomsbury, 2020.

Studios (recording and electronic)

Goldman, Jonathan, Fanny Gribenski, and João Romão, eds. "Opening the Doors of the Studio." Special issue, *Contemporary Music Review* 39 (2020). Features articles on electronic music and recording studios by the editors as well as Stefanie Alisch, Andrea F. Bohlman, Martin Brody, Brigid Cohen, and Alexandra Hui.

Meintjes, Louise. *Sound of Africa! Making Music Zulu in a South African Studio*. Durham, NC: Duke University Press, 2003.

Scales, Christopher. *Recording Culture: Powwow Music and the Aboriginal Recording Industry on the Northern Plains*. Durham, NC: Duke University Press, 2012.

Radio

Baade, Christina L., and James Deaville, eds. *Music and the Broadcast Experience: Performance, Production, and Audiences*. Oxford: Oxford University Press, 2016.

Taylor, Timothy D. *The Sounds of Capitalism: Advertising, Music, and the Conquest of Culture*. Chicago: University of Chicago Press, 2012.

Yasar, Kerim. *Electrified Voices: How the Telephone, Phonograph, and Radio Shaped Modern Japan, 1868–1945*. New York: Columbia University Press, 2018.

Streaming

Dhaenens, Frederick, and Jean Burgess. "'Press Play for Pride': The Cultural Logics of LGBTQ-Themed Playlists on Spotify." *New Media & Society* 21 (2019): 1192–211.

Johansson, Sofia, Ann Werner, Patrik Åker, and Gregory Goldenzwaig. *Streaming Music: Practices, Media, Cultures*. London: Routledge, 2018.

Siles, Ignacio, Andrés Segura-Castillo, Mónica Sancho, and Ricardo Solís-Quesada. "Genres as Social Affect: Cultivating Moods and Emotions through Playlists on Spotify." *Social Media + Society* (April–June 2019): 1–11.

Index

FILM MUSIC
A Very Short Introduction
Kathryn Kalinak

This *Very Short Introduction* provides a lucid, accessible, and engaging overview of the subject of film music. Beginning with an analysis of the music from a well-known sequence in the film Reservoir Dogs, the book focuses on the most central issues in the practice of film music. Expert author Kay Kalinak takes readers behind the scenes to understand both the practical aspects of film music - what it is and how it is composed - and also the theories that have been developed to explain why film musicworks. This compact book not entertains with the fascinating stories of the composers and performers who have shaped film music across the globe but also gives readers a broad sense for the key questions in film music studies today.

'Kathryn Kalinak has emerged as one of the freshest and most authoritative commentary on film music of her generation.'

Michael Quinn, Classical Music

www.oup.com/vsi

FOLK MUSIC
A Very Short Introduction
Mark Slobin

This stimulating *Very Short Introduction* throws open the doors on a remarkably diverse musical genre, with a world-wide reach that goes far beyond America's shores to discuss folk music of every possible kind and in every corner of the globe. Written by award-winning ethnomusicologist Mark Slobin this is the first compact introduction to folk music that offers a truly global perspective. Slobin offers an extraordinarily generous portrait of folk music, one that embraces a Russian wedding near the Arctic Circle, a group song in a small rainforest village in Brazil, and an Uzbek dance tune in Afghanistan. He looks in detail at three poignant songs from three widely separated regions--northern Afghanistan, Jewish Eastern Europe, and the Anglo-American world--with musical notation and lyrics included. He goes on to sketch out the turbulent times of folk music today and tomorrow, confronting new possibilities, frameworks, and challenges.

EARLY MUSIC
A Very Short Introduction
Thomas Forrest Kelly

The music of the medieval, Renaissance, and baroque periods
have been repeatedly discarded and rediscovered ever since
they were new. In recent years interest in music of the past
has taken on particular meaning, representing two specific
trends: first, a rediscovery of little-known underappreciated
repertories, and second, an effort to recover lost performing
styles. In this VSI, Thomas Forrest Kelly frames chapters on
the forms, techniques, and repertories of the medieval,
Renaissance, and baroque periods with discussion of why old
music has been and should be revived, along with a short
history of early music revivals.

THE BLUES
A Very Short Introduction
Elijah Wald

This VSI provides a brief history of the blues genre's main movements and most influential artists and gives a sense of the breadth of the blues field. Beginning with the music's roots in African and African-American styles, European folk music, and popular forms such as minstrelsy and ragtime, it traces how blues evolved over the course of the twentieth century as both a discrete genre and a basic ingredient in virtually all American pop styles from jazz to hip-hop.

FILM
A Very Short Introduction
Michael Wood

Film is considered by some to be the most dominant art form of the twentieth century. It is many things, but it has become above all a means of telling stories through images and sounds. The stories are often offered to us as quite false, frankly and beautifully fantastic, and they are sometimes insistently said to be true. But they are stories in both cases, and there are very few films, even in avant-garde art, that don't imply or quietly slip into narrative. This story element is important, and is closely connected with the simplest fact about moving pictures: they do move. In this *Very Short Introduction* Michael Wood provides a brief history and examination of the nature of the medium of film, considering its role and impact on society as well as its future in the digital age.